Bridge of Light

*Tools of Light
for Spiritual Transformation*

Bridge of Light

Tools of Light
for Spiritual Transformation

LaUna Huffines

Book One
The Awakened Life Series

H J Kramer Inc
Tiburon, California

Published by H J Kramer Inc
P.O. Box 1082
Tiburon, CA 94920

Editor: Nancy Grimley Carleton
Cover Art: Copyright © 1990 Ki
Cover Design: Jim Marin-Pixel Media
Composition: Classic Typography
Book Production: Schuettge and Carleton
Manufactured in the United States of America.
10 9 8 7 6 5 4 3

Library of Congress Cataloging-in-Publication Data
Huffines, LaUna.
    Bridge of light : tools of light for spiritual transformation /
LaUna Huffines.
        p. cm. – (The Awakened life series ; bk. 1)
    ISBN 0-915811-50-2 : $9.95
    1. Spiritual life–New Age movement. 2. New Age movement.
I. Title. II. Series.
BL624.H84   1993   93-37300
131–dc20   CIP

*This book is dedicated
to all of you
who are courageously creating
a path of spiritual illumination.*

To Our Readers

*The books we publish are our
contribution to an emerging world
based on cooperation rather than on
competition, on affirmation of the human
spirit rather than on self-doubt, and on the
certainty that all humanity is connected.
Our goal is to touch as many lives as
possible with a message of hope
for a better world.*

Hal and Linda Kramer, Publishers

Contents

CONTENTS

Foreword by Sanaya Roman

I first met LaUna in 1983 through a friend who wanted me to meet a wonderful woman who was teaching classes and writing books. Little did I know I was about to meet a friend who would change my life. During our first meeting, Orin, my guide, talked to LaUna of the importance of the work she was doing. He told her that she would bring through a series of books that would teach people how to work with light and other esoteric techniques. These tools would allow people to create what they wanted more easily, align with their higher selves, and manifest their life purposes. Orin told her that a very high guide had been working with her for many years to prepare her for this work.

Several months later, I had the honor of being present when LaUna's guide, Jaiwa [pronounced Jahwah], made his first appearance. Jaiwa's presence had been growing more apparent to LaUna during the writing of her first book. I felt Jaiwa's presence as waves of compassion and love. Meeting Jaiwa was a very uplifting experience.

Jaiwa is here to assist us in discovering and carrying out our world service – our higher purposes and the special contributions we came to make. He provides ways to bring our personalities into alignment with our higher selves, giving us wisdom, courage, and power. Jaiwa's gentle, loving, and penetrating insights guide us to love and value ourselves and to trust our visions and paths.

Jaiwa gives us tools of light that open up new choices

for us. These choices allow us to feel more joy and give us the power and freedom to manifest our dreams. The wisdom he presents assists us in expanding spiritually and gaining a greater mastery over our lives. The number of people working with Jaiwa in classes and seminars continues to grow dramatically. These tools of light have made such a difference in people's lives that Orin and others asked LaUna to make Jaiwa's work more widely available. I am happy that Jaiwa's love and guidance are now accessible to even more people through this book.

It is a joy to work with Jaiwa and LaUna. I have the deepest respect for both of them. My friendship with Jaiwa has greatly enriched my life, and LaUna has been a wonderful example of how to live a life filled with light, laughter, and true caring for others.

Foreword by Orin

Greetings from Orin! I am honored to introduce Jaiwa, a being of light filled with compassion and love. He is the teacher and spiritual guide who has guided LaUna in creating this book, and we have much respect for him in our realms.

You may be feeling the higher vibration of energy and light that is pouring into the planet during these transformative times. It is no longer a question of bringing in more light but of understanding how this light may be affecting you and learning to use it to grow spiritually and create the life you want. Jaiwa is here to teach you tools of light you can use to work with these new energies, and this book lays the foundation for his work. He gives you many processes, techniques, visualizations, and words of love to assist you in having more joy, inner peace, self-love, and loving relationships. These are the tools of light we use in our dimensions to create results, and they do work.

Using these tools of light will greatly accelerate your spiritual growth and personal transformation. They will enable you to stay calm and centered, follow your higher vision, and increase your vibration so that the world you experience is more positive and loving. Whether you are a novice or very advanced on your spiritual path, these tools will help you awaken a deep inner knowing of how things are done in the higher realms and how to create the life you want more rapidly and joyfully.

The application of these tools is infinite. You can use

them to improve important relationships, to discover your life purpose, and to create a higher future. You can use them to launch your business or career and bring yourself opportunities and contacts with people who will help. You can use them to balance and stabilize yourself, to create more inner joy, and to flow with the universe.

Jaiwa is here to empower you to awaken to your greater potential, open your heart, and become more radiant, alive, and vibrant with the light of your higher self. You will feel Jaiwa's love and compassion as you read this book, for he is here to show you how to have the best life you can imagine and to recognize the beautiful person you already are.

Preface

Since the first edition of *Bridge of Light* was published by Simon & Schuster in 1989, letters have poured in from readers around the world wanting more information. Hundreds of readers have also shared stories of the dramatic and transforming effect of creating their Bridge of Light. They describe finding a real connection with their soul, healed relationships, new careers, and healed lives. Many have reunited with beloved friends after meeting them on their Bridge of Light. So much more is now available to offer you that we have completely revised this new edition to include additional ways to enable you to go much further in your spiritual transformation.

The purpose of this book is to provide you with the tools of light to discover, link, and merge with your soul, and to develop the qualities that make your life a wonderful spiritual adventure. Part One is your guide to creating a Bridge of Light to your spiritual Self and experiencing it as a living entity with a transcendent and glorious reality. You will learn how to spin a Bridge of Light to courage, love, and joy, and how to bring others to your Bridge of Light to establish a connection with them from the heart and soul. In Part Two, you will learn tools to help you begin to create your new life. Part Three will show you how to create your highest possible future as you bring all of this new light into your life.

A radiant angel named Jaiwa is the true author of this book. For many years the presence of this angelic teacher has been a great source of joy, of learning, and of challenge. Bringing through these processes for *Bridge of Light* involved reaching up to the frequency of this angelic teacher, listening quietly, and then faithfully recording Jaiwa's teaching. When I align with Jaiwa's expanded consciousness, I experience such a profound depth of wisdom, understanding, and compassion that I welcome the opportunity to share all that Jaiwa is revealing with those of you who are awakening to or already participating in this rare cycle of human transformation.

You, too, may have experienced an inner teacher or a teacher from the angelic dimensions. When you were speaking to a group, writing in a journal, or working with a group, you may have recognized that some greater intelligence was revealing new understanding and wisdom to you. Think about the ideas that have been most influential in your life—the ideas that gave you new goals and possibilities, inspired you when you needed deeper answers, or embraced you with love when you most needed encouragement—and you may realize that an invisible angel was with you.

As you read, ask for the angel who is watching over your life to work closely with you. Each time you travel upward to your Bridge of Light, this angel will assist you in creating the future your soul intends for you—a life filled with joyful discoveries of your true essence as divine, vastly intelligent, and loving, with a clear vision of your highest possible future.

LaUna Huffines

Acknowledgments

Many people have generously contributed to this book in unique and creative ways. I especially want to express my heartiest gratitude to:

The Tibetan Master Djwahl Khul whose extensive esoteric wisdom is presented in the Alice Bailey books.

My early spiritual teacher, A. A. Taliaferro, who showed me with infinite patience and wisdom, how to open the doors to a truly wonderful life.

John Enright who gave me a deep understanding of the human personality and its amazing streams of consciousness as we taught together around the world.

Hal and Linda Kramer, my publishers, who have had a clear vision of the importance of this teaching for a long time.

Sanaya Roman, my faithful coworker and dear friend, for her encouragement and valuable suggestions.

A Welcome From Jaiwa

We are in a time of great revelations for humanity as an extraordinary light flows into the planet. Possibilities are coming into view to create a new reality – of peace, harmony, cooperation, beauty, and joy. Never has humanity been so desperately in need of spiritual light, and never has there been such a wonderful opportunity. This is the ideal combination for transformation – need and opportunity.

Until now, the experience of one's innate divinity has taken a long and arduous climb. The soul's vast creative love and wisdom were not purposely withheld, but it was difficult to reach from the dense vibration in which humans lived. Only small numbers of people were able to make the jump to such high vibrations. Now, with the intense light flowing into this planet from the higher planes, hundreds of thousands of people are reaching these higher states of consciousness.

Just as healing waters run deep underground for thousands of years and thus retain their purity, so does the wisdom in the higher frequencies of light surface at key transformational times with its healing and regenerating springs of knowledge and wise guidance. The ageless wisdom is being revealed more completely than ever before in response to the tremendous development of the human mind. Watch for the spiritual revelations that lie behind the words of the poet, writer, and speaker. Each one may have a different point of focus – astrology, philosophy, psychology, religion, health, politics, or finance – and the method of presentation will match the age of the soul being reached; yet whenever you feel awakened, stimulated, and enlightened by a poem, a book, or a speaker, you are touching the same shining essence that is behind all true spiritual knowledge.

The spiritual tools of light in this book are intended to give you the power of connecting with the soul qualities you want and making them a natural response in your life. Pain and suffering were tools of transformation in the past. Now your mind is so well developed that you can create your spiritual transformation through spinning a Bridge of Light to the illuminating energy of your soul rather than through the painful ways of the personality.

As your will to create a new life with your soul becomes very stable and strong, your soul must respond and assist you. When you join with your soul and let its truth, wisdom, and love become your truth, wisdom, and love, you can find answers to your most searching questions: Who am I? Why am I here? Where am I going? No situation or circumstance can block your quest to find your true source of light and merge with it. This is a cosmic law. Nothing can interfere with this law.

You can build a new life and a new future, regardless of where you are starting from. No matter how old you are or how young, how sophisticated or unsophisticated, you can make great progress in this life and achieve what might now seem impossible to you. If you have the slightest thought that the possibility exists to transform your life through making a true connection with your soul, I invite you to read further. If you yearn to understand the real purpose of your life, I urge you to investigate the path that your Bridge of Light will take you on.

Start wherever you are. You may have been meditating for years and have made contact with your soul, or you may have only now realized that you want to find a way to make this contact. If your Bridge of Light is already constructed to the soul's basic energies of light, begin there and construct the next section of this bridge. You can create the full Rainbow Bridge of Light.

As you read, ask for a greater light to assist you, and it will be there. Wise teachers will come, some who know your soul very well from the past. You are never alone when you begin to pull yourself out of ordinary human consciousness and ride a shooting star into spiritual love and pure light. You may prefer reading the book straight through without stopping to experience fully the guided journeys at the end of the chapters. If so, we invite you to order the tapes of guided journeys and meditations listed in the back of this book so you may enrich your experiences on your Bridge of Light.

Ahead of you lies an ongoing adventure of soul awakening. Begin to anticipate the changes in your life as you gain the skills to create harmony where it was missing, to be creative where you felt restricted, to experience love where indifference existed, and to be surprised by joy again and again. These are a few of the possibilities you may experience as the finer substance of your soul flows into your mind, emotions, and body—and shines outward to touch all of the people in your life.

Part One
Your Bridge of Light

About Part One

Part One serves as your guide to creating a Bridge of Light to your soul, the Essence Self. First you will explore the Temple of Light as your spiritual home for this work, and then you will learn to spin a Bridge of Light to your Spiritual Self and experience it as a living entity with a transcendent and glorious reality. Your enthusiasm and delight in life will grow as you spin your Bridge of Light to courage, love, and joy. You will bring beloved friends and others to your Bridge of Light to freely receive gifts of the spirit present there. Each time you meet with another soul on your bridge, you will receive blessings in the same generous spirit that your soul gives to others. Each of you will be enriched with new aspects of this energy—finding a more beautiful harmony together and a new sense of vision, appreciation, and love.

Prepare to experience greater light from a place deep within yourself as an abundance of soul qualities pours forth into your life. Begin to anticipate gaining the courage to create harmony where it was missing, to be creative where habit has taken over, and to experience miracles through the clear eye of wise love. These are just a few of the changes that will happen as you construct the Bridge of Light to the love of your soul and allow this love to flow into your mind, your emotions, and your body, finally radiating out to touch all of the people in your life.

Chapter 1
The Temple of Light

A beautiful and sacred place has been prepared for you to begin your spiritual journey. It is called the Temple of Light, and it radiates with the power, peace, and serenity found only in the higher frequencies of light. This temple is permeated with divine love. The atmosphere in and around it is pure and clear, far removed from the dense energies of the material plane. Each time you come into this higher vibration of light, you receive energy from the rays of light in your temple. It forms a pathway to the aspects of your being that have been beyond your awareness so that you can consciously use this vast knowledge, compassion, and higher wisdom in your life now. The Temple of Light is a sacred place to restore your inner hearing and open your inner eye to know your true Self as divine and immortal.

Your Temple of Light is a place for creative work—your sacred place from which to move out of the past and into the future. The energy here enables you to connect with the ideas and ideals that can free you from the challenges that you face today and to build the inner poise to find and to carry out your life purpose.

In the center of your Temple of Light burns a small white fire that later blazes upward into a beautiful blue and white flame. This temple can handle tremendous illumination as the flame burns brighter and is fed by your soul. This fire does not burn you; it builds, restores, and renews. This flame will begin to grow into a transforming Solar fire in the next chapter. This Solar light stirs up a profound passion and deep love within your heart. It dissolves wounds of hurt and disappointment, grief and loneliness, and the love that lies within your centermost being can finally be expressed in the world.

You can reach your Temple of Light through using your creative imagination in response to the pulsating rhythm of your higher will. As you sound the note of your silent call to your soul into the atmosphere, it responds with its own note. You begin a communication that becomes richer and ever clearer as your active imagination leads the way to the soul's sound.

When you arrive at the temple and step inside, you may realize that you have been here before, perhaps in a vivid dream or in a meditation. As soon as you enter your temple, its energy calms and clears your mind. Only then can you realize how fuzzy and unrelated many thoughts are on the denser physical plane. Working in your Temple of Light builds a storehouse of expanded awareness – valuable knowledge of reason and wisdom.

The grace of the design of your Temple of Light can give you great joy as you shape the electromagnetic particles of light to mold the temple into a beautiful structure that reflects the purity and power of your soul. Whatever is most harmonious with the energy of your soul appears as you think of it. There is no limit to the beauty of this space. Your imagination can include majestic lines, textures, and colors as you return again and again to the temple and its gardens.

Sometimes, you may come to your temple and find that

it is much larger than you remembered, or you may discover a brighter light radiating from the center. The ceiling may be very high, as in a cathedral, or open with sunlight pouring through to warm the room. The walls may change from alabaster or marble to transparent crystals. Some days you may prefer an open place of sacred energy without a form. The walls and ceiling may dissolve while the sacred space of the temple remains as powerful as ever. Other days, you may bring back a structure as a symbol for the protection and strength that it gives to you. When you replace the walls and roof of your temple, you can bring new splendor and beauty, perhaps this time becoming aware of a reflecting pool in front and a powerful waterfall near the garden.

You may also become aware of sounds and fragrances in your temple that bring harmony to your mind and body— temple bells, chimes, birds singing, and celestial music. You may fill your temple with the sacred sound of OM and return to hear the continuing reverberation of OM in your temple permeating your whole being so completely that each heart- beat feels synchronized with the heartbeat of your soul. Sub- tle fragrances may waft into your temple, providing an easier path for your soul. The unmistakable fragrance of roses may shift to the sweetness of orange blossoms, English lavender, or lotus.

The time you spend in your Temple of Light dramati- cally affects the other parts of your life. The temple becomes the meeting place between the director of your personality and your soul as your Bridge of Light sparks the soul to help you build a new life. You have a truly sacred place for spiritual transformation as patterns of light cascade into your temple.

You can build a rich tapestry of experience and expansion in your Temple of Light. It is created by a state of super alertness—hearing a sound with the inner ear, breathing in the rhythm that brings you closer to the soul, and seeing with the inner eye a sweeping vision that includes the past, the present, and the future all at once. Several dimensions may appear to be stacked on top of each other, yet each dimension is individually distinct so that you can sense it separately and as a whole, while understanding the interrelationships of the various dimensions. Your higher mind receives a transmission of wisdom and love.

With the intense waves of light that are pulsing into the atmosphere, you have an unprecedented opportunity to draw close to your soul and to see from its greater perspective, to gain from its vast experiences on its plane of existence. Your temple is the ideal place for this inner expansion. You will learn in the next chapter how to spin the connecting link—the Bridge of Light—from yourself to the soul and to bring Solar light into your temple, which transforms whatever it touches.

Journey to Your Temple of Light

Flashes of inspiration, ideas, and images are usually quite brief and rapid (often a fraction of a second). You can learn more easily to perceive and *remember* them by describing these ideas or images in a special journal after each of the journeys in this book.

You can record this guided journey to your Temple of Light and play it back while you close your eyes and relax. Or, if you prefer, we have recorded a series of guided meditations and journeys to assist you in experiencing a fuller version of the journeys in this book. These journeys on audio tape do not exactly duplicate the ones in the book; they are deeper and more expanded. For more information on the tapes, see the ordering information at the end of this book.

Begin your journey by taking several very slow, deep breaths. As you breathe, relax the muscles in your neck, shoulders, stomach, hips, thighs, and calves. Imagine that your muscles are perfectly tuned, with just enough tension to support you, like the strings on a finely tuned Stradivarius violin.

Let each breath start deep in your stomach, then expand your rib cage and fill your lungs. Feel the air moving into your stomach the way water fills a vase, from the bottom up. Pause briefly and exhale slowly, so gently that your breath could bring to life a flame from a tiny spark glowing in twigs. After each breath, pause briefly before inhaling again.

As you begin to breathe more deeply, transport yourself to a beautiful meadow covered with brightly colored wildflowers. Create the flutter of the monarch butterflies, listen to the whir of the hummingbirds, and inhale the sweet fragrance of wild jasmine and the pungent smells of juniper and pine. A mountain stream is running through this meadow as it cascades down into the valley. Dip your hands into it and taste its pure, sweet water. Look up to the top of the mountain beside this valley and identify the path that winds to the top. You will find the trail just over the small wooden bridge where you cross the stream.

Begin to climb. You can move slowly, savoring each turn of the path with wildflowers blooming at your feet and small animals scampering to safety. Or you can rise to the top more quickly by imagining yourself there.

Imagine what your temple will be like—a magnificent architectural gem with open skylights, or a simple structure with one great room, closed to the outside world. As you reach the top of the mountain, you find yourself sensitive to its finer vibration, which illuminates the whole area.

When you find your temple, before you approach the entrance, make a gesture with your hands or head that symbolizes your recognition of this temple as an unfinished masterpiece that is still under construction, and your commitment to add to its light, its beauty, and its power. Before you step inside, decide that in this temple you can learn the deeper purpose of life and begin to understand who you really are and why you are here.

Walk around the temple before you enter, until you become accustomed to its electromagnetic energy. As you shift your inner creative vision into its higher vibration of light, look for the main entrance. Notice its texture, color, and shape. Look on the door for the carved letters surrounded by symbols, and trace them with your fingers. You may feel as if they have been there for a very long time, hand carved in times that you have forgotten.

Grasp the door knob and slowly turn it until the door opens. Step inside the entrance, and behold your temple, shining with an inner light, quiet, peaceful, and in harmony with your soul. Look at the ceiling, the windows, the walls, and the floor, and notice the details of each before you move into the center of this room. Listen for the temple chimes and bells.

There may be beautiful colors already apparent, or you may wish to add these. Make each color pure and transparent. Brighten or soften the colors to harmonize with the space. There may be short bursts of light or a luminous glow as if from within the walls.

Choose an area from which to do your work with the light. You may want a chair or soft cushion. Add other furnishings, such as a lovely desk, a beautiful gemstone, or anything else that complements the temple. You may wish to face the east. Notice which direction this is.

Invite the energy of the higher beings or guides of humanity, the invisible teachers from the inner planes. Assume that your soul is fully aware of your presence and why you have come, even if you cannot yet perceive its vibration clearly. Much can become visible to you here that was hidden before. Just sitting here in total stillness—receptive, open, listening—you may sense areas of your life where you are pressuring yourself unnecessarily or activities that are draining your energy without actually serving you or anyone else. You may spontaneously become aware of people who are teaching you or supporting you with love regardless of how far away they live.

You also may envision, if you ask, a picture of your life as a wondrous journey of expanding consciousness that reveals how every experience is teaching you more about loving, giving, and receiving.

From this clear place of higher perception, ask to sense the single most important focus you could hold this week—whether about your life, a relationship, or your career. If there is a challenge in your life now, ask for an inspired awareness concerning the highest action you could take to handle it, and to assist someone else as you do so. Ask to become aware this week of those moments when you are responding to a higher vision of your life.

Your temple is your base camp for a wonderful journey into greater light and joy. Honor it as your sacred place of wisdom, truth, serenity, and love. As you experience an inner strength and balance, you can carry this with you back to the physical world, with an expanded ability to handle any situation in your life with a new poise. You can come back to the temple anytime to deepen this expanded sense of yourself. When you are ready to return to the temple, touch your right hand to your heart and imagine returning. This touch alone will bring you back into the sacred temple whenever you wish to come. It is the signal to transport you to your temple in an instant. Remember, you do not have to "see" a temple—only to raise your consciousness until you sense a sacred place of spiritual expansion within you.

As you fall asleep tonight, you can enter into an altered state where creative solutions or inspired ideas come to you. As your ordinary self-consciousness shifts to a dual consciousness of self and Higher Self, take advantage of this state and go to your Temple of Light before you reach this threshold state of sleep so that the greater light can illumine your sleep. Not only does sleeping in your temple offer a window to see more clearly; it also allows you to experience yourself as a larger Self without boundaries of time or space. You can go to sleep at night in the temple and take advantage of hours of learning from those who are guiding you. Gradually, you can train yourself to bring back some of your experiences while you are in your temple as you sleep.

Chapter 2

Constructing Your Bridge of Light

Creating a Bridge of Light illuminates you and your life; it links you with the soul so that you can experience its wisdom and love in ever increasing degrees. The bridge you are creating forms a permanent link between your personality and your soul. As you connect it to more and more aspects of your soul, this bridge radiates with every color, each translucent and shining. It becomes a Rainbow Bridge of Light.

To build this bridge, you will be spinning filaments of light out of the substance of love from the center of energy near your heart. These filaments will be as strong as steel, indestructible yet quite flexible. You can return again and again, creating and discovering new destination points. In time, you can take yourself to the exact aspect of wisdom or love you need at any moment.

Many people have created miracles on their first venture onto the Bridge of Light. One man, whose grown daughter had rejected his love and would have nothing to do with him, met his daughter on his Bridge of Light to try to persuade her to get in touch with him. But when he met with her in the radiant light of their Essence Selves, he suddenly realized that he had been terribly dominating, controlling, and possessive. He was shocked and dismayed to recognize this, and he tearfully asked her forgiveness on the bridge. The next morning, his daughter contacted him and came in love to reunite with her father. Their tears revealed how deep their forgiveness was and how rich their new soul connection.

Even the hardest hearts begin to melt and a greater wisdom emerges when the soul's light is touched. Several stories have come to us of business and professional people who pretend to object to considering the power of the soul as a real force in life, yet who are "closet" bridge builders. They secretly listen to the Bridge of Light tapes when no one else is at home and apparently derive deep fulfillment from them. Others tell of being hailed by a patrol officer who intended to give them a ticket. During the wait for the driver's past record, they created a Bridge of Light and met the officer's Essence Self on the bridge. In each of these cases, the officer had a change of heart, and no ticket was issued.

You build your Bridge of Light to the soul plane. Those who have higher clairvoyant sight can see when this link is made. The teachers and guides of humanity can see the Bridge of Light. You can also sense its added strength at each step, and then cross it to meet your soul on the other side. There is no reason to wait until you have released your physical body to meet your soul and to merge your energy with it. You need its higher intelligence, its light and power, right here and now.

There are many names for the soul: the Self, the Higher Self, the Spiritual One, the One, the God within, the Essence Self, the Christ within, the Angel, the Flame of Spirit, the Director, the Observer, the Divine Perceiver, the Watcher, and the Interpreter.

The soul is most definitely not an image created in fantasy

or a symbolic way of finding hope. It is not a defense mechanism or an escape from the very real problems of the present. The soul is an intelligence that has created your mind and emotions with pure spiritual energy through vibration and love; it has used the physical substance of the earth for your body. The soul possesses all truth, wisdom, love, divine will, and creativity.

Your individual soul is a conscious, living entity with its own body – the light body. It is the child produced when spirit and matter meet. Its vibration, or note, becomes clearer, purer, and more refined as it gains enough experience to begin its return to spirit. Each individual soul is in rapport with the soul of all things; it is an integral part of the World Soul, aware of the purpose of humanity, the planet, and its other lives here. It intelligently cooperates with the will of the Creator and works with the plan of evolution.

Your soul sets its long-term purpose and sponsors your life here to gain knowledge and experience. It sends a fine thread of light and anchors it in the heart to give life to the body. Then it sends a second strand of light into the head to give consciousness to the body. Both threads are broken at the time of death, when the soul is liberated from life on the physical plane to return to its own plane.

Your higher will and your awakened love for humanity activate your decision to find and honor this source of greater love within yourself. Your soul waits for you to spin a Bridge of Light to it and make your way to its higher frequencies of light. Even though your soul has extended its light to create your life here on Earth, it lives in a much finer frequency of light. Its very nature does not allow it to enter fully into this level of density.

You can connect with your soul every day, each time increasing the passageway or channel between your personality and your soul. Its intelligence activates your dormant brain cells and gives you an urge to gain new understanding of who you are and to find the higher purpose of your presence here on this planet. The dynamic, energizing, life-expanding force of enlightenment can come only from the soul.

As you construct the Bridge of Light to aspects of the soul that are closest to the higher mental plane, this level may seem at first to include "all that could possibly be." Yet there are higher aspects of the soul and its source that will be accessible in time as you continue to strengthen your bridge. To build your complete Bridge of Light, you spin filaments of light from the substance within your heart and head centers and gradually weave these together to extend this bridge to even higher planes.

Building links to the soul and the light beyond the soul is an ongoing process. Gradually, your Bridge of Light comes to extend to different dimensions of your soul, giving you access to the knowledge, love, and power your soul has gained through ages of experiments and experiences. These qualities are energy patterns, each with its own note and color. When your personality perceives these energy patterns, it gives them a name—such as love, wisdom, joy, beauty, harmony, enthusiasm, trust. By spinning lines of light to different qualities of your soul, you gain the ability to use these qualities on the physical plane, expressing them in your physical life with every contact and situation. You can bring more of this light into your life each time, until eventually every part of your personality is touched by its power of transformation. Your mind and thoughts, your feelings and emotions,

16

your physical body – the energy in all these parts of your personality – are gradually transmuted to provide the path for your true spiritual life through your Bridge of Light.

Once you have made your first real connection with your soul, it begins this transmutation in earnest and sends more of its energy into your mind and body. With your soul as guide, you begin a journey that transforms your life. The changes may seem gradual as you are spinning these strands of light to the soul, yet they add up to a profound expansion that affects every relationship and area of your life. Having your soul's intelligence to guide you does not automatically solve all problems, but it does show you what you can do to solve them. Even when it is necessary to proceed blindly through a problem in your relationships, your family, or your work life, each strand of light that connects you to a facet of your soul's shining essence offers tremendous assistance in revealing the next step, and the next, until you find yourself standing free of confusion or obstructions. Rather than planning an escape from a difficult situation, you are empowered to go to the center of the problem, see how to unravel it, and take the wisest action. Your action becomes soul directed rather than an effort to escape pain.

Activating Your Highest Creative Faculty

Your active, creative imagination is the first building substance for the Bridge of Light to connect the conscious mind and the higher mind and soul. The impulse to build this bridge originates from your soul as an active desire to embrace the highest part of yourself. All progress is self-initiated. Your commitment calls forth a response from the soul, for its vibration to travel along waves of living substance to begin your spiritual transformation.

As you build your Bridge of Light, materials are supplied to you in abundance at your request. How is this possible? You are working in the etheric and mental planes. They are as real, but much less dense, more flexible, and infinitely abundant. The one requirement is that you oversee the construction, and continue it each day or so by rising as high as you can on your Bridge of Light. When you begin the journey, use as pure a substance of love as you can to link your heart center to your head center. Let your bridge be so filled with light that it shines with infinite beauty, color, and grace. It must withstand all storms and high winds. Let its destination be sure, so that you can take many journeys into the hidden realms of spiritual realities.

For you who like to think in less abstract terms, envision this Bridge of Light spanning the space between the top of the spinal cord, past the brain, to the intelligence of a yet unexplored part of your being that has communicated up until now only with your higher, or abstract, mind. On the etheric plane, you are extending the bridge that connects the energy centers at base of the spine to the heart, throat, brain, and higher mind. You are setting up a communication system to connect all of these to your soul, from your conscious mind to that intelligence and wisdom that lies beyond the conscious mind.

The diagram here shows two triangles, the personality and the soul, with the Bridge of Light connecting them. This diagram is simplified to present the different aspects of the personality and the soul.

You are ready to create the first span of this Bridge of Light. Prepare for profound shifts in your Self-awareness.

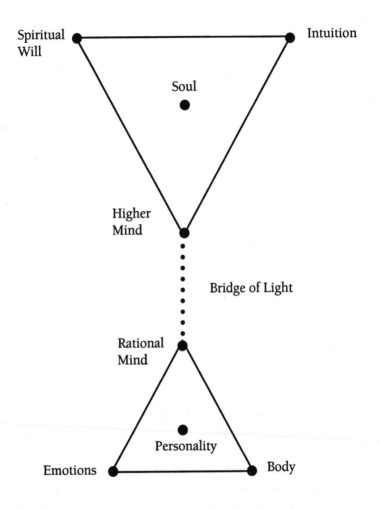

What once seemed painful you can now transform into a deep sense of power through compassion. You can now activate unfulfilled dreams of an "awakened" life that were temporarily blocked.

A Journey: Constructing Your Bridge of Light

Find a place where you won't be disturbed for twenty or thirty minutes and sit in a comfortable chair. Loosen any tight clothing and begin by taking several deep breaths as you relax the muscles in your body. Notice the thoughts in your mind, and then let them go. Notice your emotional feelings, and then let them go, too.

Guides of a high evolutionary grade are assisting you as you begin to construct this Bridge of Light. They are strengthening your efforts to place yourself consciously on the path of light.

Walk across the meadow of wildflowers and climb to the top of the mountain to your Temple of Light. Say the sacred word OM three times. The first time, imagine that all of your emotions are focused on the higher rays of light. The second time you say the sacred word, focus all the neurons of your brain on reaching the vibration of your soul. The third time, focus your whole mind on reaching your soul. You may sound OM silently or aloud.

Open the door to your temple, inhaling deeply as you stand in the entrance to immerse yourself in the atmosphere. Open to receive the shimmering light into your heart. Let it penetrate the cells of your body and mind. Continue to breathe deeply until you are quite serene and tranquil.

Open your mind and heart to imagine how your life might be different if you had the soul's light to enlighten your path each day. Imagine your new Self-image as if this Essence Light were infusing spiritual energy into your life, forming a network of connections to love, wisdom, truth, humor, patience, compassion, joy, and beauty. Imagine the wondrous adventures that await you on the Bridge of Light when you find a rich network of translucent tunnels of light to the places of true wisdom and love!

Choose a specific soul quality you want to develop. Perhaps you never thought of yourself as light and humorous and would like to bring that quality to your life. You may want to develop patience, serenity, and harmony, or to find beauty within and around you. Understanding, inspiration, enthusiasm, love, or vision may be the most important to you now.

Imagine a great ball of light somewhere in the vast universe of higher consciousness that is the emanating source of the quality you have chosen. Breathe into your heart center of love several times, and imagine that each breath is opening and expanding this part of you. Next, spin a strand of light from your heart center (located a few inches away from your body slightly below your shoulders) to the radiating energy of the soul quality you have chosen. Spin it to the center of this quality.

Create another stream of light with each breath, then another, spinning each stream of light one by one until all the streams of light link you with the brighter light of your chosen quality. Add more streams until you feel the connection is made. Feel yourself rising toward this magnetic energy of the soul. Think about the quality whose vibratory patterns you are appreciating. What would this quality mean if it were in your life every day? How would your life be different? How would you know if you were completely infused with this quality?

Give permission for the vibration and color of the soul quality you chose to flow into your mind and heart. Breathe deeply to draw this energy into your whole being.

Speak the name of the aspect of the soul that you are reaching toward, and repeat this name aloud very slowly. Feel the stronger connection through the sound of its name. Write the name in large letters of gold on the screen of your mind.

Stay as long as you like. If you repeat your journey to this same quality several times before choosing a new aspect of the soul, it will begin to form a pathway of light in your head and heart. With practice, you can rise up on this Bridge of Light and refresh your mind and heart in the middle of a long day, restore your good humor, and enjoy a poised state of higher awareness.

When you are ready to build a bridge to another aspect of the soul, decide which quality would enrich your life most and focus on reaching its vibration as you begin to spin new lines of light into your Bridge of Light. You can build this higher contact with your soul without "seeing" an actual bridge leading to it. Simply hold the intention to create the connection and imagine yourself rising into the soul's light. Remember, in the spiritual realm, everything is a metaphor to assist you—a kind of map that points you in the right direction.

Building a Bridge of Light to Radiant Qualities

You are ready to begin exploring new destinations within your soul's body of light. As you build your Bridge of Light to courage, love, and joy, you are connecting with the major soul qualities that are needed to integrate the higher waves of energy that are moving into the planet. Unexpected changes can happen as you infuse these qualities (and others) into your life. You may begin to sense yourself as a timeless being, an Essence Self rather than a personality. You may experience a new beginning.

Your children and your friends also receive these spiritual gifts as you develop them in your consciousness. The gifts allow them to courageously expand into greater light through love and joy by natural inheritance. The child you once were, who still remains a part of you, is also transformed as you do this work. Experiences of loneliness and fear as a child, or any other unhappiness, cannot be healed with personality techniques alone, no matter how clever the methods. Only the soul has this power to transmute and to transform. Just as ordinary electric lights cannot supply the nutrients to permit a tree to blossom, flower, and produce fruit, when the tree is outdoors and the rays of the sun reach it, fragrant flowers and fruit grow in profusion.

A personality has a dim light compared to the light of the soul. Like the sun, the soul transmits a completely different quality of light, one that nourishes beyond present scientific understanding. On your Bridge of Light, you can touch the same essence of light that the sun transmits to the planet, although you reach a gentler vibration of this Solar fire that your physical body can handle. Every dimension of this light acts as an extraordinary healing and transformative agent.

You can build this bridge with so much light that you can bring others from anywhere in the world to your bridge to receive its blessings. Before you meet with others physically, imagine them standing on the bridge with you as you absorb its healing essence. Later, when you are with these people on the physical plane, recall how they appeared in your imagination in their light bodies. Remember how you related on the Bridge of Light and hold this picture in your mind. Their response may be silent, but the spirit behind whatever you do together is very likely to be motivated by a new sense of appreciation and cooperation. Sometimes you may both experience a moment of inner harmony that is so deep that words cannot express it.

Until these qualities are infused from the soul on the Bridge of Light, you may experience a tendency to be in pain if a friend is in pain, to be insecure if friends are insecure, to have fear if someone around you is fearful. So long as the link between you and others is a personality link (vulnerable to every wind of fortune or change) rather than a soul link, you may at times feel discouraged or helpless. Most people do. But anytime the soul link becomes stronger than the personality link in a relationship, a new hope arises, a new direction begins, and nothing is ever quite the same again.

Through infusing the vibrations of all lighted soul qualities into your mind, emotions, and physical cells, your beliefs change and your heart center expands. A sense of forgiveness for past mistakes (your own and others') may occur. Gradually, you will experience less attachment to personality reactions and more interest in the soul quality that overrides a negative reaction to a person or a situation.

Chapter 3

Connecting With the Power of Courage

Many beautiful souls have come to us wanting practical information about the next step on their paths. It becomes clear that they are filled with excellent ideas and have the skills to begin. They need only one additional element: courage—the courage to listen to the soul's silent signals, to assess their strengths, to speak up or to be silent according to the time, to step forward even if others say stop, and sometimes to stand still when others say go.

At times in your life, you may have had a dream of finding some way to get the courage to live from the wisdom of your soul. The inner desire to reach higher and live from a state of light may bring new challenges. It is as if the soul sets up a situation that requires more courage to handle, and your commitment is tested. All tests are set up by the soul, and they are entered into with your permission even if you don't remember giving it. Tests provide the means for progress, and each test calls for a new type of courage—not bravado or brassy behavior, but wise and deliberate action.

Courage is one of the most important qualities for making your dreams come true, for preparing yourself for the expanding work that you came here to do. Your courage to express the greater wisdom and love of your whole being can assist many people in finding their paths, including some whom you may never know you have influenced or inspired. The first dramatic shift after you bring in courage is a new surge of life energy. You get the energy to follow your desired direction. Or for the first time you see the possibility of giving a high priority to spiritual growth.

When you imagine the essence pattern of courage, you may find that it is a sister to fine mental discrimination and the spiritual will to move forward. True courage requires a steady and persistent action to make the right turn when you meet a crossroad on your path to light. Each time you act with courage, you empower your entire life and change your future. The courage you express in any part of your life spreads to other areas and finally permeates every thought, every word, and every deed. You begin to empower others; as they see your persistent, patient will to choose the path of light, they find new hope and inspiration for their own lives.

You can safely assume that your first act of courage was when you (as a soul) decided to create a material body that could live on this planet, to gain more experience and expand into a finer light body. You left the security of a higher consciousness to risk the chance that the personality you created to handle the material plane would somehow remember who it really was and why it was here. With your analytical, discriminating, wise power as a soul, you also knew that you could expand and serve others by working closely with your personality. As the soul, it was your intention to use all of the skills you had learned through your long soul life for the needs of those who are lost and suffering.

As a personality, you need not be a Joan of Arc or a Galileo to express your soul courage. You have shown courage

many times – in emergencies, during crises, and at critical decision points – often forgetting all about your personal desires
or safety in order to intervene for someone else. You may
be able to look back now and see some of your courageous
acts. These are clearly recorded in your energy field as turn-
ing points in your life. They were the times when you took
a step toward becoming what you knew you could be as a
result of an inner vision. You may have done this in spite
of strong objections from family or friends, removing yourself from an atmosphere that was pleasant but that kept you
lulled into a kind of sleep.

Acknowledging Times of Change

Think of one or two of these periods of your life that
were leading you into spiritual expansion, times when you
ignored the fear of being criticized or looking foolish. Your
courage was stronger than your fear. You used your soul's
higher power of discrimination and made a conscious choice
to expand into more light.

You may have moved into new beliefs, shifting your
awareness to a higher level of who you were. Or you may
have moved into a new physical location, perhaps without
money, job, or family. Often the two go hand in hand; a physical move may follow an expansion of consciousness. Adding
a room to your home or creating a garden is also a symbolic
act that creates ripples outward. Even painting the front door
to your home a new color can serve as a symbol of courageously acknowledging a new dimension of who you are.

Speaking and acting with courage may look different for
each occasion. One day you may use courage to create a deep

friendship or to create family harmony. Another day you may use it to leave behind financial security or the comfort of family and neighborhood friends. Each self-initiated change takes great courage. Familiar ways are nearly always the easiest to follow. A new honesty in expressing the light within you takes courage in every situation, and the more practice you have, the more natural it becomes!

Your Cosmic Chronicle of Courage

Imagine which acts in your life might be recorded in a cosmic chronicle that contains a detailed record of your courageous decisions and acts. In this chronicle are recorded those times when you refused to take the easy or familiar path and responded with courage to a higher calling that came from within your heart and your deep mind. Such courageous acts may not have taken place in one dramatic moment, but they nevertheless embodied decisions that changed the direction of your life. You may not have felt especially courageous when you made these choices. You may have felt trapped or scared to death. Others may have considered you disobedient, rebellious, or just plain stubborn. But you took the courageous step anyway.

When you act with courage, you may not realize you are being courageous. It may seem that you are simply doing what you feel you must do. True courage is built by acting on the insights and inspirations that you receive in your Temple of Light and on your Bridge of Light. Regardless of outside barriers, you can move steadily forward with confidence and grace, fully assuming your right to do so, just as you assume your right to walk freely up the street in your town.

When an essence quality such as courage is still an unopened flower, you can assist it to open to full flower by looking for opportunities to express it, no matter in how small an arena. Even the most minor event where you use courage begins to build confidence and poise for the next opportunity. Often one of the most courageous acts you can perform is to express gratitude to others for being who they are, to tell them how much you learn when you are with them. You express courage when you hold a vision for friends to awaken to their innate power—while not telling them what you are doing. When you complete a responsibility that you know is rightfully yours, even though it is very difficult and challenging, you also embody courage.

The fear of being criticized or looking foolish may have stopped you in the past, but as you absorb the frequency of courage to enable you to speak truthfully, you come to see that courage is never foolish. Being impetuous, acting before you think, or unloading anger on someone else is usually foolish; it may be an honest emotional reaction, but it is not courage. True courage results from a steady and persistent reflection on the wise way to handle a situation and from then carrying it out, always with the intention of bringing greater light to each life involved.

Strengthening Your Link With Courage

The purpose of this exercise is to assist you in recognizing fear the minute you begin to tighten up mentally or physically. Exaggerating these two stances of fear and courage sets a trigger in the back of your mind, so that whenever you are withdrawing from the action you know you should take, you can remember how it felt to be crouched in the corner of the room and choose the opposite stance. Learning to identify tension building up when you are trying to avoid pain is the first step in accessing soul courage.

1. Start by standing in the center of the room and pretending to feel fearful and cowardly. Crouch down in fear. Exaggerate this posture, your hands stretched out to defend yourself, your body tucked in tightly, every muscle tensed, your neck strained as you look upward for protection. Notice the tightness in your chest, the difficulty in breathing freely. Observe every muscle strain, even around your jaws and eyes. Relax and move to the other side of the room.

2. Now, rising to your Temple of Light, stand in the vibration of spiritual courage and assume the physical and emotional posture of courage. Stand very tall, very poised and balanced, with your head straight, your muscles at ease, your mind at peace, and your emotions calm. Notice your breathing deepen and your eyes become sharp and alert. Hold this stance long enough to memorize it. By simply taking this posture in a difficult situation, you can access courage in a flash. The posture opens the door for the soul's light to flow into your mind and body.

3. Affirm that you are abundantly flowing with the vibration of courage. Affirm that courage is entering your circulatory system, becoming a part of the biochemical component of your blood. As you affirm this, it will be so. Breathe in courage and breathe out confidence. Repeat the word *courage* with each inhalation, and repeat the word *confidence* with each exhalation. The deeper you are breathing, the more these qualities can penetrate your cells.

Every time you act from courage, you strengthen your ability to live by the authority of your own soul. Speaking honestly where you have felt compelled to cover the truth, speaking audibly where you have been silent, being silent where you have spoken without compassion—all of these acts require courage. And as you explore new possibilities that once seemed beyond you, you have taken the first step—and you are motivated with courage to take the next step that is being revealed right in front of you.

Courageous actions build greater confidence and help you reach farther out. Success creates more courage until you can sail through the very situation that once caused you to contract in fear. The quality of courage can deeply affect even your later years. At sixty-five or seventy years of age, you may feel so spirited that you learn a new skill, such as swimming or playing a violin. You may discover that your mind is quicker and brighter at seventy-five than it was at forty, and you may take advantage of your mental skills by studying biology or psychology. You might begin to write a book or teach, whatever your courageous and inquiring mind turns toward.

Anytime you become very clear and committed to something, you can find the courage to do it. Courage is easier when you have a sense of higher purpose. The courage to say no, to say yes, to begin again, or to let go of something that is superfluous in your life comes when you experience a real sense of purpose in doing so. One volunteer worker to help feed the hungry in the cities learned that the very poor he was trying to help had broken into the vans carrying the food and stolen it. It took courage for him to continue pouring his energy and money into that section of New York when it seemed like a lost cause. Yet he received a clear impression from his soul of how important this work was, and he redoubled his efforts until he had enough volunteers to distribute the food fairly through local churches. This group of volunteers has spread to every major city and by government request has even expanded to other countries.

Chart Your Deepening Courage

Use this exercise to compare your courage now with your courage five years ago. Use the following chart to set the level of courage you desire six months from now on a scale of one to ten, with one representing a very small level of courage and ten meaning an outrageous expression of it. Consider even a one point increase a significant step forward.

1. Fill in today's date so you can see the improvement the next time you look at your chart. Before you fill in the last column, stop and imagine how it would feel to express courage at the level you desire. If you can imagine it vividly enough, you can do it.

2. If you have not yet realized that you are beginning to express courage, reflect on the six opportunities to express courage listed and see how far you have come. Each experience (including that of delight) can increase your courage to act from the power of your soul.

3. In two weeks, check the chart again and notice the areas where you are making new leaps in courage. Acknowledge your progress to one or two friends, and another demonstration of wise action will be free to appear.

4. Keep a journal of all acts that required new courage if you would like spiritual courage to become a habit. Each time you allow the light of your essence to flow into your life, you are integrating another level of courage and making this new level more available to others—including both people you know and people you don't know. Courage is a wonderfully contagious quality!

Courage Chart

Today's Date _____

	Five years ago	Now	Six months from now
1. Courage to ask your Higher Self to show you everything that stands in the way of your highest expression.			
2. Courage to say no to requests for your time or energy that you have no interest in.			
3. Courage to meet with your Higher Self and to open to its love and wisdom.			
4. Courage to acknowledge a beautiful trait in someone, even someone you do not know well.			
5. Courage to consciously allow pictures to emerge that represent the future closest to your heart and to believe in those pictures.			
6. Courage to see yourself as a radiant being of light.			

Blending Courage With Other Soul Qualities

When a conflict arises or a challenge presents itself, there is additional power in synchronizing one soul quality with another. If your job is threatened by a coworker, for example, you may need courage, but you also need truth and compassion to handle the situation in a way that is straightforward while also embued with true understanding. When you envision becoming much more effective in your work or more loving in your relationships, you may need several qualities along with courage before you can act on your vision.

1. Select a situation where courage would make a real difference. Transfer the energy of this situation from your mind to your left hand. Make this image vital enough so that you can feel the situation warming or vibrating in your hand. How would this situation change with courage added to it? Decide how you will know when enough courage is available.

2. When the desire to bring courage to this situation is very strong, begin to spin a Bridge of Light to the great intelligence that radiates patterns of courage with intense rays of light. Imagine yourself in your essence body moving across the bridge several times, each time bringing the light of your heart and connecting it with courage at the other end of the bridge. On each journey, leave another trail of light behind to strengthen your Bridge of Light to courage.

3. Imagine your body and mind filled with the essence of courage. Taste its distinctive flavor. Close your eyes and say the word *courage* to yourself each time you cross the bridge. Imagine that this energy is entering your circulatory system and penetrating all the cells in your body. When you feel your pulse beating with the vibration of courage, place this energy in your right hand.

34

:ond soul quality, such as understanding,
;, or serenity, and construct your bridge to
'. Each quality has its own individual pat-
:t this pattern flow into your mind and body
Now add this quality to your right hand.
;o add humor and love—or whatever other
most helpful in this situation. When you
1ulsing through your heart and head, send
1r right hand as well.
1ve brought together the energy of several
distinctive healing qualities. Hold your palms in front of you,
facing each other, and slowly, very slowly, bring them closer
together. You may sense an invisible energetic field between
your palms as they get closer.

7. Gently bring your open palms together until they are
touching, each finger matched with the same finger on the opposite hand. Hold your hands together for a moment or so as
you close your eyes and inhale deeply while the lighted neu-
ron transfers take place in your brain.

8. After a few minutes, imagine the situation and observe
any changes. Notice how you might handle it differently now.
Using your creative imagination, take yourself into that situation and play it out in your mind using your new patterns of
light. Notice what happens.

9. You are symbolically bringing the qualities into the situation that lift it into a higher plane where greater clarity is available. New ideas may continue to surface in your mind as you
go through the day. Note these. The qualities you have brought
into your body and mind are now available to use in similar
situations as well. Gradually, they will spread so that they are
available automatically in any situation that calls for courage,
understanding, love, compassion, and all of the other qualities you have merged together to handle challenges.

Chapter 4

Experiencing the Expansive Energy of Love

Spiritual love is the essential nature of your being, awaiting the powerful streams of light from your soul to be fully expressed in the material world. As you absorb the vibration of love from your soul, an entirely new spirit may flood into your mind and emotions. You can enrich this love with every breath you breathe in the awareness of love's miracles of transformation.

Every life form is held in place by this vibrant, expanding force. Its vibration underlies all physical existence. The highest vibrations of love offer great rewards, automatically creating order, harmony, expansion, and beauty in every life form—from a single atom to a whirling galaxy of stars. Love is the ultimate healing force of the universe. Its expression causes the evolution of planets, humans, animals, and plants. Soul love is the place where mind and heart meet with spirit and bring forth the finest traits within each life form.

Just as the sun breaks up a dense fog, a Bridge of Light to love clears the atmosphere, revealing hidden beauty in yourself and in everyone else. When you construct lines of light directly into the force field of divine love, a major transformation begins. You may sense this substance as golden particles of light flowing into your mind and body. These particles have a powerful healing effect, reaching deeply into your mind and heart and shifting the whole atmosphere of your home. When you are immersed in these golden patterns, others are inspired to rise to a higher state when they are with you. They reach up to match your expansiveness, and they cannot help but sense some of the beauty of their Higher Selves, even when no words are spoken.

Spiritual love feels joyful as it moves through you and out to others. If love ever feels like a burden, an obligation, or an effort, it is time to stop and regenerate yourself on your Bridge of Light. Receiving love from the higher dimensions is as important as giving it out. Both giving and receiving must be in balance. If talking becomes an effort or you suddenly feel very sleepy or tired, this is a sign that you have begun to borrow on your essential stamina. It is also possible that the person you are with has reached his or her limit of receiving. No one wants to receive more love (or anything else) than he or she can return—the scales are not balanced and disharmony results.

Expressing Soul Love

Expressing soul love is free and leaves others free also. You may not always receive from the same people you give to, but by cosmic law you always receive greater blessings of love than you can give. The rich actually do get richer— when love is the value for wealth. Expressing love creates a larger container for more spiritual love to flow through you.

The love that you give to others affects you as powerfully as it does those you give it to. Every time love flows through you to someone else, it also moves into your body and permeates your emotions. This process begins a deep healing of old regrets, guilts, griefs, and mistakes. One layer at a time, the energy of love flows into your mind and emotions and heals them. It flows into your past and into your future, giving nourishment to the small dark corners, sweeping all debris to the surface to be disposed of. It is as impersonal as the sun, shining its vital life energy upon everyone and everything. This may sound mystical because there are no scientific terms to identify the higher vibration of love, but its actual substance will someday be established, and scientists will finally identify it as an agent of healing and regeneration and give it a respectable scientific name.

One woman learned the tremendous power of love when she realized that a brilliant college friend had somehow given into despair and had been drinking to numb himself from the pain. She was tempted to scold, argue, threaten, or sympathize with him in the name of love. Instead, she brought her friend to her Bridge of Light to love and surrounded his essence with a golden fountain of light. She did this many times after their phone conversations, never mentioning to him what she was doing. Several weeks later, he called to say that he had never been a religious man at all, but that something very strange and wonderful had happened. He was lying on the couch and suddenly realized that a powerful and unmistakable "presence" had entered the room. This presence was clearly benevolent; he could see this presence above him as a luminous form that, he decided, must be some kind of angel. It hovered over him for a few minutes, and then, moving toward his body, merged right into his heart. At that moment he felt very different all over. His mind was at peace, his ever-present anxiety gone, and an inner stillness gave him a deep sense of serenity. Since then, he has not been interested in drinking and has begun to rebuild his life. The Bridge of Light had brought this gift to him. By meeting in the vibration of spiritual love, the bridge builder had chosen a higher love than her personality could offer and brought her friend to the fountain of love that heals all souls regardless of the circumstances.

Helping her friend was this woman's main objective, yet she received as great a healing within herself—recognizing how much value she could offer to others through her Bridge of Light. Now she is building her bridge with greater commitment than ever before and also teaching her friend how to build his own Bridge of Light.

This woman now knows from her own experience that there is no light or dark to soul love, no shadow side, no separation. There is only identification with the heart of all love. The closer you can identify with the soul, the more love can flow through you to others and create the links that unite all people. This is different from the beliefs about love found in many relationships, including family relationships. In personality love, one person may wander into a dense fog and drag along the ones he or she desires to serve. Many good people are bewildered and imprisoned by obligations that are not theirs through their limiting ideas and ideals about love. There is much confusion about love and the desire to receive affection. The desire to receive affection produces a controlling relationship. The one who controls is the one who has less need to receive affection.

You have probably assisted friends in shifting into a state of higher awareness, new hope, vision, or clarity. Perhaps you were not aware of exactly how the shift happened. Often, when soul love is activated, the personality is not yet aware of it. You may have simply spoken briefly or offered a hand quite naturally to others, while the impact of spiritual love was leaving an unmistakable signature of light on their souls.

Creating a Bridge of Light to Soul Love

1. Take time to get very relaxed and comfortable, perhaps lying back with your eyes closed. Release the day's concerns and all sense of being busy or rushed. Enter your Temple of Light, and move into the serene and tranquil space here.

2. Begin to construct your Bridge of Light to love, spinning filaments of light to the highest level you can imagine. When your bridge is ready, walk out on it and stand in the center. Begin in the soul's anchoring places—your heart and head—and link these two energy centers with your breath. You will probably experience waves of energy moving across your bridge, calming your emotions, your mind, and your muscles. These waves of energy hold the secret of those who seem eternally young and whose eyes reveal joy quietly dancing in their hearts.

3. Imagine that you can see yourself only as patterns of color and light. Some of these colors may be brighter and clearer than others. Some patterns may be geometric and organized, and others may be less clear. Look ahead to one year from today and see how these patterns have changed. Notice which colors have become brighter, more translucent, and more beautiful. You can also peep further into the future, five or even ten years ahead, and perhaps get a sense of the changes that will have taken place. Even though you are only imagining you can see these changes, it is your imagination that gives permission on a deep level for soul love to make greater changes in your life.

4. In this vibration, you can release many expectations about love that were based on personality desires rather than on the power of spiritual love. Look closely at all obligations in your life and notice which ones are yours and which you have taken on that truly belong to someone else.

5. Decide how you can create the atmosphere to express the love that is sounding its note within you, how you can express lighted love from the notes of your own soul as a unique and original expression of spirit.

6. Now imagine your soul group—that combination of souls that your soul has come into incarnation to learn from and join with in service. See this group growing in brightness and beauty, strengthened by the activated soul love you are sending. See its powerful imprint infused into this group of souls, even though you may not yet have met them on the physical plane. This kind of shift—leaving a whole group feeling joyous, strong, and centered—happens easily when you gather with your soul group on the physical plane and you all meet in the illumination of soul love together.

Chapter 5

Drinking From Your Spring of Joy

Joy is the keynote of planet Earth. Each of you is a part of the plan to bring joy to this planet. You have heard the note of joy many times when you have created a picture of what the world would be like if peace and harmony reigned here, or if goodwill became supreme among all people. You may have heard the note of joy in your sleep as a lingering sound within the heart, a beautiful melody playing itself without an instrument.

You may have given up trying to make yourself feel joyful–and wisely so. Joy comes from creating order and harmony and beauty, and when it comes there is no stopping it. Joy is the natural response to any soul contact–with your soul, with that of a friend or teacher, or with the World Soul itself.

Watch for joy darting in and out of your awareness; listen for its quiet approach. Like a cool breeze on a warm day, it may come up from behind when you least expect it, playful and spirited, making you want to laugh out loud with delight in simply being alive or to smile at the realization that you (and everyone else) is seeded with the light of the Spiritual Sun.

Joy exists at all times in the core of your being. Beneath the surface of the feeling of happiness or unhappiness, pleasure or pain, serenity or struggle, flows joy. It flows underground and can suddenly burst to the surface, much as deep springs bubble up with pure water that has been running underground for thousands of years.

You may have held joy back in an effort to be a spiritual or serious person. Yet, once you give your full permission, joy can break through even the most rigid pictures and present itself as a sense of pure delight, profound gratitude, and expansive discovery. Even if joy has gone so deep underground that it seems to have vanished, eventually it will find a way to the surface when the cover is lifted. A courageous or compassionate act can lift the cover. A friend's welcoming smile, beautiful music, a child's wonder, a puppy's warm tongue on your cheek—these and many other experiences can melt the resistance that has held joy back.

Placing Joy in Your Path

1. Take your calendar and mark it for three joyful days in the next month. Randomly select these three days, and write a brief description of the kind of joy you intend to experience. Form a very strong picture of how much delight you will experience on each of these days. You won't need to set up the circumstances; leave that to your wise Self, which can get through all doors that you open to it. But it is important to imagine yourself grinning from ear to ear, feeling so light and humorous that life seems like play—productive play, yes, but still play. Or imagine yourself dancing around the kitchen, or waking up laughing out loud, simply in response to joy.

2. Give at least two weeks' notice for your first invitation for joy, and space the other two days well apart. You are learning to increase your limit of experiencing joy—the one that your parents inadvertently set by their own limits. Many times your

loyalty to your mother or father is so strong that even after they are dead you cannot allow yourself to experience more joy than they had. Once you realize this, you begin to free yourself from rejecting that which they would have wanted you to have more than anything else in the world.

3. Spin a Bridge of Light to joy and stand in the center until you can feel a lighter sense of yourself. Bring these three calendar days to the bridge. Imagine that you are holding each of these days in the palms of your hands and that a vibrant, pulsating energy of joy is permeating each day! Then forget all about what you have done and go about your day. Joy may come in ways that you least expect; your mind may create an outside reason, yet the true cause of the joy is that you have, for that one day, lifted the cover that usually holds it back. Regardless of what is happening around you, you can be surprised by an experience of joy. These experiences grow stronger and more frequent when you set them up in advance. You are removing old habits that covered joy for that day—and soon joy becomes a wonderful new habit.

4. Mark your calendar to give advance permission to experience other soul qualities, such as serenity, trust, beauty, or oneness, and see what happens!

A Journey to Share Joy With Your Friends

As your joy grows in strength and becomes more stable, it begins to permeate you with its specific vibration, leaving its imprint on whatever or whomever you touch. When this joy bubbles up, its imprint is as distinct and unique as your signature. You absorb the rhythm and sound of joy; your voice carries its rich overtone. Others may recognize this sound emerging in your voice before you do. The overtone is registered on the inner ear and responded to from the heart. Rather than try to make your voice *sound* joyful, you can embrace a symbol for joy and absorb its sound in the following journey.

1. Begin by engaging your imagination as you take a relaxed position in your Temple of Light. Recreate your Bridge of Light to joy and walk on it. This time, walk closer to the originating source of joy, that intensely bright and clear light that your bridge is connected to. Imagine that joy is ringing you with concentric circles of light. Each circle has the vibrations to reach different groups of people in your life. It is charged with the qualities that transform sadness and break up the habit of looking backward instead of forward. Let the colors and energies of each circle first cleanse your own emotions and then clear your inner sight and hearing. Feel the passion rise in your heart—the passion to learn, to work, to serve, to grow spiritually.

2. Select one of the symbols for joy that are stored deep in your higher unconscious mind. This symbol might be a flower, a star, a tree, a bird, or the sun, among others. Bring this image closer to you so that it can become an agent of joy. Speak to it and let it speak to you, telling you how you can help it grow larger and stronger. Let its radiance increase.

3. Create a circle of family, friends, and acquaintances. Let these people stand shoulder to shoulder facing the center. You can have as few as four or five or as many as one hundred in this circle.

4. Turn slowly to face each person individually and create a line of light that carries the joy you have received from the soul on your bridge. Use your symbol for joy and let it touch the head and heart of all present, lifting their spirits, shifting their thoughts and feelings to a finer dimension.

5. See each person receiving to his or her limit, and then

move on to the next. Imagine these people going to bed tonight with a lingering sense of peace in their hearts and a new sense of hope about the future. Even though you are creating these groups to give back something of what you are receiving, the truth is that you are receiving more than you can give. As you expand your ability to give, you simultaneously expand your ability to receive. This is an immutable law of the universe!

Chapter 6

Bringing Others to Your Bridge of Light

You can meet others on your Bridge of Light—friends, family, employers, even whole groups of people with whom you wish to connect soul to soul and share some of the blessings of the bridge. One woman was in a state of deep sorrow because her path was so different from her husband's. He was a prominent surgeon and she was an artist. The intention and purpose behind their work seemed so far apart that she felt a deep loneliness and isolation on her spiritual path. As she walked on her first Bridge of Light, which she had spun to the living quality of compassion, she discovered her husband approaching her from the other end. As they met in the middle, they embraced and reconnected wordlessly. She felt such a healing love from him that a great weight dropped from her shoulders. She realized that although he did not speak in "spiritual" terms, he was as dedicated as she was to finding ways to add something valuable to people's well-being and happiness. As she described her experience, her face softened to reveal a hidden beauty and youth. Her voice dropped to a melodious pitch as she spoke of someone she loved very deeply.

Another woman was creating her first Bridge of Light and carefully walking to the middle when she saw her mother standing there waiting for her. This woman had grieved deeply ever since her mother had committed suicide when she was a small child. In spite of years of therapy to get over the trauma, she felt that her mother had betrayed her and also that she had somehow caused her mother to take her life. Yet the figure that stood before her was unmistakably her mother, looking very joyful, young, and radiant. She communicated to her daughter in an instant of time why she had taken her life and all that she had learned since then. They embraced in pure joy. For the first time since that event, the woman experienced herself free from this terrible burden. She discarded old patterns of trying and failing to succeed and began a business of teaching people how to create success in their careers. From that moment on, her world became filled with happy people, and the depression she had known for many long years never returned.

When you meet others on your Bridge of Light, they are not only present in your imagination – the higher parts of their being are present in reality. One woman brought her brother to her bridge to love, hoping to heal a deep split in their relationship. When they met in their light bodies on the bridge, she told her brother that she accepted him just as he was and that all past divisions were forgiven. Then she returned to her Temple of Light. A few weeks later, her brother called and spoke to her with great warmth, expressing the love they had known before their split several years before. The healing had happened without long discussions and explanations. It was as if the hurts had never existed. On your Bridge of Light, anything can happen. Healing can occur in an instant; love can be restored in a flash of time.

Another woman walked out on her Bridge of Light to

wisdom and invited an old friend to join her, not for any special reason, just to connect soul to soul. No words were spoken as they met there, but the woman experienced a sense of being surrounded by the shining light on the bridge. In a few days, her friend called her and shared an inspired plan that changed the career of the bridge builder. They had met on the Bridge of Light to wisdom, and now her friend was showering her with a gift she had never dreamed of receiving!

On your Bridge of Light, you are in a state of balance, poise, and equanimity, identified with the radiant energy of yourself as a soul. The other person is drawn to this light and sees you as your Essence Self. The personality may not remember the episode, but the soul knows. The other's soul is stimulated by the contact with your soul, and the meeting filters into the conscious mind soon after. Whatever veils of the personality have hidden your Essence Light from the other person start dissolving. A complete honesty may unexpectedly break through. And the truth of the actual love that exists between souls becomes – for that timeless moment – stronger than either personality's reluctance and actual inability to hold another person in the higher light.

Often, you may experience a silent, yet very clear, communication coming to you from the essence of another person on your bridge to love or your bridge to joy. Somehow you both stand naked, revealed to each other without the personality habits of self-centeredness, mistrust, or separation. The link of all souls can be seen, and in time you can see that no one is entirely separate from you. You may sense that you, as a soul, are a fragment of the great World Soul, and so is everyone else.

Each soul has a mission, a purpose, and a focus, just as your own soul does. Every time you make a contact with another soul on your Bridge of Light to any lighted soul quality, that soul is stimulated to send more energy into the life of that person. It isn't necessary to give any instructions or suggestions to the soul.

You can help many people by bringing them to the Bridge of Light with you. The process takes only a minute and can provide a great lift to their spirits—even when they have no idea that you are doing it. Each time you offer this light to another soul, everyone is blessed. No matter how hard you try, you cannot bless others more profoundly than the blessings that come to you when you see your community of family and friends as radiant beings of light who are clothed in colorful personalities.

A Journey: Constructing
a Bridge of Light to a Friend

1. Select a significant relationship that is profoundly affecting your life now, even if the other person lives far away or is no longer in a physical body. You can choose someone whom you admire or appreciate but do not feel truly connected to. You can choose someone you have never met or someone you have known for a long time.

2. As this relationship with someone else is deepened and enriched, you are simultaneously establishing a connection to some part of your personality that has been isolated in some way from your soul. There is no need to think about this dual relationship shift. It happens all by itself.

3. Close your eyes and breathe as you did when you

created your first Bridge of Light, letting your breath fill your stomach and then your lungs as your rib cage expands. Exhale and imagine that you are releasing all impurities. Repeat these breaths until your hands become warmer and your breathing takes you into the center of your Temple of Light.

4. Now bring the soul quality of love into your breath and imagine that you are inhaling pure photons of golden light as you breathe. Feel your heart center opening as if it were made of rows of petals and as if your breath were coming from the center of these petals. Visualize strands of light permeated with the highest love you know being spun from the substance of this center. See your life force propelling these strands upward as they form a bridge of golden light.

5. Send these strands of light to the originating source of love in the highest dimension. As they reach their destination, they quiver for a moment as the higher vibration pulses into them, and then their color will become translucent. You don't need to see these changes; they happen just the same. When you have spun many of these strands of light to love, anchor this bridge firmly to your Temple of Light and walk out on it. Experience the unique patterns of beauty here, and observe the difference in yourself as you reach the center.

6. Invite your friend to your Bridge of Light. When she or he appears, it is in essence form. Your friend is standing beside you in a light body just as you are. Time does not exist here; there is no sense of rushing. Words do not exist—there is nothing to say—although you can communicate with ease. Just be here together, allowing your light bodies to touch or even to embrace. Observe how your friend's light body expands with you on this bridge that is connected with the source of love. You may also discover a sense of unity in this profound spirit of truth. Let it happen. You are absolutely safe on this bridge.

7. When your meeting is complete, and all communication has been given and received, return to your temple to reflect on what has happened and to offer gratitude for this contact with the energy of pure love—the ultimate transforming and healing ray of light.

Part Two

Creating a New Life

About Part Two

Congratulations! You have climbed the mountain, entered your Temple of Light, and created the first three sections of your Bridge of Light to your soul–courage, love, and joy. You have spun lines of light to these soul qualities, brought a friend and a group of friends to the bridge, and surrounded them with Essence Light and joy. Now it is time for the practical work of handling problems, challenges, or crises that come up in your life as you bring these waves of light into it.

Part Two includes techniques to help you understand the sides of yourself that have held you back, and to help you retrain these sides of your personality to fully cooperate with your transformation. You will practice breathing soul energy through words of light, using an essence detection device to discern which goals are personality desires and which are soul inspired. You will also learn ways to handle fears, to use challenges and crises as spiritual doorways, to build in the lighted emotions and thoughts you want, and to keep a balanced and sane mind as you accelerate your spiritual transformation.

All that you contact on the inner planes, all that you focus your inner eye upon, will find its way to your outer world. The real test of all spiritual work is not whether you have had a conscious experience of your soul, but how your life is expressed in the everyday world–with family, friends, and coworkers. The true effectiveness of the Bridge of Light is determined by your will toward positive action and your steadfast focus on the inexhaustible light that shines from within.

Chapter 7

Breathing as the Soul

The ancient wisdom is correct: Expand your breath and you expand your life. You provide a path for the higher frequencies of your soul when your breathing rhythm is in harmony with these frequencies. You may already have noticed that your breath becomes more peaceful when you are in your Temple of Light. After you leave your temple, you may feel energized even if you felt tense or tired when you first entered the temple.

The more open your breathing, the more easily you can imbue your personality with the greater light of your soul. When you breathe in the awareness of yourself as a divine being, there is another unmistakable result. A spray of light flows into your mind, like the spray of a fountain with hundreds of thousands of tiny drops falling through the air, reaching into unexpected places and events, sometimes creating an inner smile, sometimes a moment of expanded awareness.

Not only does the truly natural breath facilitate your birth into greater light, it opens new windows to perceive the world. Although it may seem automatic and purely physical, how you breathe creates different filters through which you see yourself and others. Certain patterns of breathing give you sadness, others give you a sense of futility and anger, while others lift you into delight and a sense of playfulness or fill you with creative ideas and ways to put these ideas into action.

Shallow breathing exists anywhere there is a sense of competition. Yet when breathing is shallow, the brain does not get enough oxygen to be creative. Short bursts of breath create tension and make life look like a struggle. They propel the brain into fast frequencies and set up a pressured feeling, even when you are trying to relax. Because shallow breathing creates rapid, short brain waves, it causes feelings of being behind and needing to rush. Grim overseriousness gets in the way of opportunities for happiness. The immune systems of shallow breathers are weakened, leaving them vulnerable to illness and fatigue.

As a newborn, you breathed with your whole body, in perfect synchronized rhythm to give every cell its full nourishment of oxygen. Shallow breathing develops from the psychic atmosphere in which you grew up. It is the way to breathe to fit into the ordinary world.

On your Bridge of Light, your breath trains your brain and teaches it how to receive the truth of your being. Even as you imagine living in these realities, your breathing may begin to find its natural rhythm, becoming slower, calmer, and more energizing. It is not forced, but completely spontaneous. Gradually, the soul's breath becomes stronger and brings a creative touch even to ordinary activities.

Finding the Soul's Breath

In time, the soul may seem to be breathing you. You may notice, after a flash of insight or inspiration, or after a surge of joy or courage, that time seems infinite, the present moment stretching out, ongoing and enduring. This is the soul's breath, its rhythm and tone, taking you into its immutable and immortal home. There is an unmistakable rhythm, a depth, a relaxation, as the air sacs fill up and use more oxygen. The rhythm is relaxed and effortless, expanding the identity of who you are with finer molecules of light. With your brain fully nourished with oxygen, you feel wise. You *are* wise—for that long moment. You are inside the vibration of your soul, which has stored its wisdom in its light body, waiting only to be activated by your desire to know.

Sometimes when you are meditating, you may notice that your breathing may almost seem to stop. In reality it becomes so expansive, with rhythmic pauses between each breath, that it is barely noticeable. You may only be breathing three or four times a minute, yet this doesn't seem artificial or forced, but natural and easy. This is the breath that allows the next step to be revealed to you. Take that step, and another is revealed. Best of all, each step you see from this state of consciousness seems absolutely possible, even if you don't know exactly where to begin.

The habit of breathing with the natural breath moving into every part of your body creates a permanent switch in consciousness. Feelings of tranquillity signal that your brain waves are moving closer into phase with your soul or Higher Self. Even if you don't hear or feel anything unusual, the changes are still happening. Don't look for results each time. Expectations tend to limit the results and actually block the natural breath. Just notice that as soon as you are in your Temple of Light, a beautiful reorganization is taking place.

Emotions become calm and positive as brain waves lengthen and become more synchronized. Prompt yourself when you feel irritated or get into a rush with the phrase "Remember to breathe as the soul, remember to breathe as the soul!" Remember this one principle, and you can pull yourself out of approaching fear or panic before it arrives, simply by transferring your breath and consciousness from the personality's rhythm to the soul's rhythm.

Clearing Your Mind With the Breath

A focused and clear mind lies just beyond any mental fog you may experience, and it is only a few deep breaths away! This exercise takes from three to five minutes. Use it if your mind feels fuzzy, or if the same thoughts keep recycling through your mind.

1. With your right hand to your heart, enter your Temple of Light. Stand or sit in the center.

2. Exhale and wait until your breath comes in by itself. Pause briefly as your breath reaches its fullness, and then let it go. Rather than inhale, wait until your breath naturally comes again to fill the empty space. Use your arms to circle up and out as your breath comes in; bring them down to your side or your ankles as the breath goes out.

3. Select a beautiful word that carries the energy of your soul, and begin to say this word aloud as you breathe. Use a word that your mind and emotions and body all respond to when you say it aloud.

4. Repeat this word several times. Breathe until you feel energy dancing around in your brain. Let the vibration of the word move through your brain, from top to bottom, from left to right, from front to back.

5. Imagine your breath carrying the vibration of this word up your spinal column and down again several times, refreshing

your entire nervous system and leaving its signature of light and color as it travels up and down your spine.

6. Become the breath traveling through your nervous system and brain, energized and enriched by the essence of the word you have chosen. Feel the greater space in your head and sense the gratitude of the tiny conscious cells of your brain for the light you have brought to them.

Mental clarity and energy are sure to follow if you practice these simple steps.

One woman tried many times to force her breathing to deepen, but she always forgot within a couple of minutes, and her breathing returned to its normal rhythm. Now she goes to her temple, relaxes, and repeats beautiful words aloud. Her favorite words are *free, beauty, love, wisdom,* and *joy.* As she repeats each word, her breathing – and her mood – shift, becoming calmer and more balanced with a barely perceptible pause at the top and bottom of the breath. When her breathing shifts, her mouth softens, her face looks younger, and she feels lighter and confident about having a good day.

Several mothers of infants and young children play the tape *Creating Your Temple of Light* at a very low volume to get their children to sleep through the night. The children feel safe and secure as they go to sleep in their temples and instinctively match their breathing with the tranquil images and music.

Chapter 8
Soul and Personality Goals

How can you tell which of your driving urges to succeed, to build a special relationship, to buy land or a home, to travel, to start a business, or to change jobs are soul urges that will carry you into greater light and which are personality ambitions that will limit you from the very expansion you seek? How can you know whether you are tapping into an intuitive knowing when you make a decision, or simply following patterns and beliefs that were begun when you were very small.

When you bring new light into your life, you may sense that something terribly important is missing, something that you can't quite remember even though you know it exists. Solar light awakens this memory. It also reveals how much Essence Light is in each goal and spotlights areas where your focus can bring simple yet profound joys. The brighter light shows you where your schedule is now out of balance and awakens a strong urge to set new priorities.

The opportunity to walk across the Bridge of Light to meet your soul is unequaled by anything the material world can offer you. An abundance of money, a fine house, wide travel, a distinguished career, an ideal love or family life – the personality may consider these goals high priorities. Some of them may further your spiritual transformation as well. If not, the deeper spiritual hunger in the heart remains, eating away at the very essence of life. If your goals are only personality goals, after they are achieved, you may look back and see the utter waste of time and energy spent in the struggle to get them and say, "Thank goodness, I have time and energy left. I shall begin again."

You may want to think carefully before you set any new goals for yourself. Goals create their own patterns in your energy field. A fifty-eight-year-old man found this out forty-four years after he had set a long-forgotten goal. He was swimming for recreation one day and realized that if he swam twelve more laps he would complete a mile. He was utterly exhausted, and yet he felt a senseless and compelling urge to keep on swimming way past his fitness level. On the last lap, he distinctly recognized a message sent to him from his soul, "Okay, you have finally realized a goal you set long ago. Be very careful what new goals you set. They can take precious time and energy, and all of them must be fulfilled so long as they still exist in your energy field." It was then that he remembered a goal he had set at summer camp to swim a mile when he was twelve years old. That goal was still lingering in his energy field to be fulfilled, even though it no longer made any sense to him—and there were no ribbons to earn.

Think over the goals lingering in your energy field that are left over from earlier desires. If your goal has a deadline date, it is probably personality based. If it has pressure built into it, if getting it means that someone else will be excluded from that privilege, if it means another loses when you win— these are signs pointing to a personality goal that may actually

66

take away more than it can give. You can consciously remove these less rewarding goals from your energy field and replace them with soul-infused goals that will reward you at any age and enrich your life more abundantly every year.

Each time you construct a Bridge of Light, you are bringing the light into your mind, your emotions, and your body that invites you to embrace the goals that sparkle with this Solar light. The next step is to create the life-style to integrate and use all the light you are bringing in, to be flexible so that you can adjust your schedule to meet and embrace the vision and revelations that come to you.

Your Formless Essence

To make the distinction between soul and personality clearer, think of the snow that falls on top of the tallest mountains, pure and dazzling, reflecting the light of the sun. As a portion of the snow melts, it forms streams and waterfalls that splash down the mountainside and into the valley below. As the streams rush farther and farther away from their source, they pick up debris. The streams lose some of their sweetness and sparkling clarity as they flow to the valley floor, often slowing down and meandering around before joining together. The life of this river depends upon the continuing flow of fresh water from the melting snow. If the channel becomes blocked anywhere upstream, the water loses its sparkling clarity until a new surge of melted snow comes through and clears the channel again.

Just as the snow is the source of these mountain streams, your soul is the source of your life. Think of these streams as aspects of your personality—body, mind, and emotions—

merging to form a strong and integrated personality. The streams and later the river contain much more than melted snow; they have gathered everything in their path in their long, meandering journey around and down the mountain, just as your personality has gathered in its streams of energy much more than the pure spirit with which it began its journey.

The personality valiantly tries to compensate for the lack of essence vision. Without true vision, it creates many goals and distractions. When the personality realizes that something extremely important is missing in life and turns its eyes upward to the soul, the regenerating effect is unmistakable. Gradually, the energy of the soul increases from a tiny stream or trickle to a vibrant stream of energy into the personality. The mind and emotions become calmer, the vision clearer. New possibilities for a wonderful life come to light.

Creating Harmony Between Soul and Personality Goals

The personality yearns for challenge. The more challenging the goal, the more intrigued the personality. Personalities love to begin self-discipline programs – losing weight, becoming fit, looking younger. The personality likes to gossip, bargain, compare, and try to get ahead; it wants to be good, to be liked, to be helpful, and to be powerful. But when the goal isn't in line with the soul's purpose, the energizing rush of soul light does not flow in. Personality goals make claims on energy that is not there. The personality begins borrowing core energy with a vague promise to pay back someday. Personalities have skills and knowledge to accomplish much;

what they don't have is the panoramic view of the larger purpose of a series of lifetimes that the soul has set up.

When a goal is in response to higher inspiration, this goal vibrates in ways that give you energy rather than taking energy from you. Watch for the self-energizing projects in your life; even the most challenging ones regenerate you in some way and have an intrinsic value in your life. The goals that are half personality desire and half inspiration can also be very valuable. For example, any move forward toward a healthier life-style and a clear, orderly mind that serves you, and the group you are associated with, is energized by the soul. Whatever you accomplish tends to have a more positive effect when you set up times of inner stillness and reflection *before* you commit your time and energy.

Anytime life seems like a struggle and the same problems keep reappearing day after day, use these tools of light to remind yourself to stop and reconnect with your soul through a Bridge of Light to love, courage, joy, or any other quality that your soul contains. The minute you step across the threshold of your Temple of Light, you can immerse yourself in this healing love. The goals that were creating a sense of struggle can shift in the greater light and become a wonderful adventure of Self-discovery.

Creating an Essence Detection Device

Any work can feel selfish and yet be soul directed. A project can also seem totally altruistic and yet actually reflect a personality effort that is not the soul's work. Here is a very good tool to know the difference. It bypasses your analytical mind and gives you an imprint of your higher mind's knowledge.

Get a notebook or fresh sheet of paper and a pen. Read through the following instructions first and then do the different parts of the exercise.

1. Close your eyes and breathe deeply several times, as you relax your muscles and your shoulders. Gently roll your neck from side to side. Cross the meadow, climb the mountain, and open the door of your Temple of Light to step inside.

2. Go into your temple and imagine that you have an essence detection device that can measure the precise degree of soul light in any thought, goal, or relationship, and show this measure to you as a number, a color, or a symbol. Decide to play with the detector and ask the rational side of your mind to put down its shields and allow the superconscious Self through while you play.

3. You can picture your detector having a one to ten digital readout if you like numbers, or a gemstone brilliance scale if you like symbols. If you prefer colors, look for vivid, clear colors to reveal the essence value of the work you are doing. Expect the response to each question to be instantaneous. The answers come through your intuition and bypass your logical mind.

4. Stop reading right here and list your most important goals without stopping to censor. Place the essence detector directly over each goal and check the goal with the essence detector. Write whatever number or symbol comes to mind without stopping to think. Like any skill, the process of checking your goals for their essence quality becomes sharper and more precise with practice.

5. The essence detector can print other useful information on your mind screen. Ask for a signal light flashing red or green to show you the most likely outcome of an anticipated action or a situation you are already involved in. (Your "inner

consultant" knows far more than you may realize.) When you set up the opportunity for this intuitive knowing to come through, it will.

Transforming a Personality Goal With Light

You can take a project or goal that is personality based and transform it with a specific quality from your essence. The energy that is now flowing into your Temple of Light assures the success of this experiment. Begin with a simple, yet often resisted, task.

1. From the heart of your Temple of Light, choose a personality project, such as cleaning a closet, reorganizing your desk, or updating your wardrobe. Mentally place it in the palm of your left hand. Talk with it to firmly establish its presence in your hand. When it is in place, choose an essence quality that could make that project a delight—for example, humor, patience, clarity, wisdom, or beauty.

2. Place the essence quality you have chosen in the palm of your right hand. Concentrate on its presence until your right hand tingles or becomes warmer. Create a line of light from your Bridge of Light to your mind, to your heart, and into your right hand. Pulsate this light into your hand.

3. Next, hold your palms up two or three feet apart, facing each other, fingers together. Begin to bring your hands together very slowly, an inch or so at a time. Hold personality resistance in the left hand, and soul light, love, and power in the right hand; both carry energy patterns of their own. The energy from each hand radiates to the other one, creating a pleasant tension between them. Imagine this space as a ball of light as you move them closer together. The more slowly you move your palms toward each other, the more energy

builds up. Finally, bring both hands together and hold them there.

4. Think about the personality project again and notice how it is shifting, perhaps with a new direction or purpose, the best time to do it, and a sense of ease and pleasure in completing it. Possibly, the project now seems a nonessential project to keep yourself feeling busy or overworked. Or it may have shifted into an interesting appointment with yourself. Whatever shifts you observe will have placed this project into the right perspective. Now it can bring you far greater rewards than it could have before you infused it with the greater light of your soul.

A man in our seminar discovered that his goal of traveling to Egypt had a nine in essence energy with his essence detector. When he decided to change the date of his trip, the number dropped to two. Only then did he realize that the spiritual group and leader whom he would be with in Egypt at the earlier date carried most of the essence energy for that goal. He immediately chose to stay with the original date and group. When he returned from the trip, he was infused with a greater motivation for his spiritual work of teaching than before.

Chapter 9

Directing Your Orchestra of Selves

One of the major challenges in living in the new light is to identify what is you and what is not you, to know where your permanent Self ends and unconscious desires begin. The desires that come from some parts of your personality may already be receiving energy from your Bridge of Light. These parts of your personality support your spiritual transformation as well as they can. Other parts may be living in the basement of your life where there is little light, and they are as yet completely unaware of you as the director of your personality or your Essence Self. They were assembled to handle some challenge in the past, but their way of handling situations may no longer be in harmony with you as you bring in the finer frequencies of light. Now their efforts to help you may actually obstruct your path. All of these parts are called subpersonalities—the ones that live in the sunlight of your mind and the others who can't get to the sun until they receive assistance from you.

The subpersonality in control determines how you think and relate to the world at that moment. When a subpersonality that is not yet connected with light comes on stage, it can set into action a whole chain of thoughts, feelings, and actions that block your path to your Temple of Light. Each one has unique reactions and characteristics; one subpersonality might react with anger, another with resentment, another with jealousy, and another with plain laziness. Its criticism is meant to help, its judgments to signal danger to its own goals. When it is angry, sullen, vengeful, or jealous, it is trying to protect itself. No subpersonality is against you. If it is living in a darker light, it feels alone and is simply trying to survive. It may also want to be helpful to you, but it needs wise guidance from you to carry out its good intentions. Behind each one of your possible reactions is a subpersonality who needs to be brought into more light in order to experience the transforming power of the love flowing through you now.

Freeing Your Soul Self

If you identify with a subpersonality and call it "I," it has control over you. You give it power that it doesn't deserve. Such statements as "I am hurt and angry" or "I am in terrible shape" mean that a subpersonality has moved onstage and that you have momentarily forgotten who you are and identified with it as yourself. By giving a subpersonality a name, you separate it from a false position as your real self. You can begin to talk with it before its negative mood takes you over. After all, it did play a part to get you where you are now.

You have control over anything that you don't identify with. If you say, "There is a little part of me that feels angry" (hurt, confused, jealous, or scared), you are reclaiming the top position for yourself as the director of your personality—the one who has direct access to the Higher Self and its light. If you say, "I feel a wave of anxiety coming over me," you then have the choice to take refuge in your Temple of Light until the wave washes over you. As soon as you realize it is a subpersonality instead of your real self, you can smile or laugh as you do when you see a crazy image of yourself in a fun house mirror. Humor is a wonderful tool to heal a subpersonality.

Each subpersonality has an opposite according to the planetary law of polarities. As you observe a subpersonality more closely, you discover that there is another one with an opposing view. It may be quiet most of the time, but it exists somewhere, and it controls an equal amount of energy as its opposite. A subpersonality, for example, that feels superior to some people has an opposing subpersonality that feels inferior to others. A subpersonality that is messy has an opposite one that is neat and orderly. One that rebels against work is matched in power by another that loves to work. The procrastinator is matched by an equally potent "doer." Neither is bad or wrong, but both can waste your time and energy, leading you from one extreme to another. Yet, when you embrace both of them at the same time, they move closer together until they merge and form a very strong and useful part of your personality. When this happens to the procrastinator, for example, both it and the doer merge and become a third vibration, one that is strong because it is balanced. This vibration is a child of the two parents–and a healthy, cooperative, intelligent one at that.

None of these subpersonalities is a permanent part of your being. But until you see that they are only temporary, they may seem entrenched. They are actually neurological patterns developed in the past that have gathered enough energy to take on little lives of their own. You created most of them when you were a small child learning to cope with many different situations. Think of your subpersonalities as holograms. A hologram of a dancer looks solid. It seems to move as you walk around it, yet if you reach out to touch the miniature figure, your hand goes right through it. It only appears to be real. The solid figure is an illusion created when the beam of light projecting a photographic negative is split into two beams. Subpersonalities—even those that create anxiety or guilt—are no more solid than holograms. They represent certain patterns in the unconscious mind, just as holograms depend on patterns in the film. It's a feat of courage to let go of thinking that a subpersonality is your real self when it seems so established as a way of thinking. But the moment you disidentify from it, you are free again to act as the director of your personality, which has direct access to the Bridge of Light.

Getting Each Subpersonality to Work for You

Think of the author of your life as your soul, which has patiently waited for a very long time for its original script to be heard and followed. You are the director of the play— you are the central "I" of your life—and all of your subpersonalities are the actors in the drama. You can gradually develop excellent actors who take direction from your central personality self instead of going off in scattered directions and dragging you with them. The director of your personality always knows what to do with the soul's script.

Since all subpersonalities are created by the mind, you can coach them to use their skills in ways that are truly helpful. You can focus on any of your subpersonalities and analyze them, diagnose them, cajole them, excuse them, or berate them, but they learn best from encouragement and a new vision. Teach them to understand and cooperate with your vision and with one another. As you establish a working relationship with your subpersonalities, the special attributes of each become obvious. You can use some of them to organize your work, your physical fitness, and your time schedules. Others may enjoy the precision of words and be able to help express the ideas that come from your Higher Self. Your recognition of your subpersonalities and your willingness to get to know them and retrain them can give them the kind of nourishment they need to change.

Teaching Your Subpersonalities to Trust You

As you work with these parts that have blocked your inner joy and delight in life, they learn to trust you, and you can begin to count on them to cooperate with you. They have unique skills that have been used against you; now you can convince them to use these skills for you and the new vision you are developing for your life. Once you have established a conscious relationship with your subpersonalities, you can learn what they need from you and explain what you need from them. Soon, you can make an agreement with them. Whatever agreements you make with them are very important to keep. This process develops trust between you. These smaller aspects of your personality all possess some skill that you can benefit from once you retrain them. As you start to give them useful tasks, they begin to honor their commitment to assist you.

Subpersonalities respond very positively to direction once you have befriended them. One of the first subpersonalities you can retrain is the one that's critical or judgmental. This is the one that finds fault with the way you are handling your life and doesn't hesitate to point out specifics. As this subpersonality is transformed, the pure joy of being alive can bubble up again. In time, each subpersonality becomes aligned with your finer rhythm until you have enlisted every undermining, mischievous, impetuous, or rebellious side of your personality to cooperate with you, using all of their skills and tools.

One woman took her foot-dragging ("I don't want to do this hard work") subpersonality named Sarah up the mountain near her Temple of Light. There she listened to Sarah's complaints, her needs, and her list of desires. ("I feel chained to this work; I want to play.") She identified Sarah's skills and acknowledged that she needed Sarah's skills to help her balance her overseriousness with play. She then taught Sarah how to become a cooperating part of her whole Self. Sitting in the light of her Temple of Light with Sarah, she showed her a larger picture of her life, and they made clear agreements to work together: Sarah would add humor to her workday and remind her to stop work at an agreed hour, and she would take Sarah on delightful walks in the parks every day for at least twenty minutes.

After you have gained its cooperation, you can take each subpersonality to your Temple of Light. A man in our seminar climbed repeatedly to the top of his mountain, where the light was clear, with a different subpersonality in hand for each trip. When the soul's light was shining on it, each subpersonality made a shift into a more beautiful form. As they were transformed, in their places stood a shining knight, resplendent in gold or silver—a wonderful symbol to confirm the power of his soul to transform whatever it touches.

As a subpersonality moves closer to you, it finally merges into your personality and becomes a dynamic source of strength to you. Each newly integrated subpersonality empowers your personality to draw closer and closer to the vibration of your soul, to infuse your whole personality with this radiant Essence Self, and to express it in every situation.

Creating a Trusting Friendship With a Subpersonality

1. Select a time and place where you will be undisturbed for half an hour. Close your eyes and take several deep breaths. Let go of outside concerns. Connect with your Bridge of Light by imagining a column of light rising from the top of your head. Let it rise until it meets a column of light from above focused toward you. When the two lights are joined in your mind, become aware of your breathing again. Each deep, easy breath clears the column of light so that it is more luminous and transparent. Let your breathing be slow, effortless, and rhythmic.

2. Feel yourself rising until you are standing on the Bridge of Light, in a higher dimension than the ordinary world. Imagine that you see below you a wooded area with several little houses among the trees. Choose one of the houses to visit and imagine yourself approaching it and knocking on the door. When the door is opened, one of your subpersonalities invites you to enter. Get to know this subpersonality. Give it a name (Hazel, Jo, Rupert, Priscilla, or whatever), and begin by finding out its needs. Listen to its complaints or comments about the way you have treated it. Don't let it engage you in argument or self-defense. Be gentle and understanding. You are here as a respectful guest.

3. Invite the subpersonality to go outdoors in the sunlight and take a walk with you. As you walk, tell it your needs, and

when you feel that a trust between you is established, tell it your vision of your life and your work. Learn about its skills and how it can assist you. (For example: "Please gently remind me how good I feel when I eat only nutritious food. I would really appreciate the reminder.")

4. On this walk with your subpersonality, you have the opportunity to transfuse it with light and a new vision. As you acknowledge and appreciate its skills, watch it transform in some way. It may begin to look and act differently as you walk in the sunlight together. If it had a shriveled or hunched shape, it may grow taller and healthier. Its attitude will probably become more trusting and positive.

5. Before you leave, make an agreement to handle its reasonable needs and get an agreement from it to help with your needs. Be specific. If it wants you to exercise more, decide how much you are willing to exercise and still be in balance with the rest of your life. If it shows you that you are wearing your body out too fast, make a specific agreement about how you will take better care of yourself. This is the beginning of a very powerful process to assemble all of your energies together to empower your life.

6. Ask yourself where in your body you have kept this subpersonality lodged. Look for any tense patterns in the muscles of your stomach, shoulders, neck, thighs, or jaw. Ask the subpersonality to let go of any hold it has over your body in return for your taking it on walks or otherwise acknowledging its needs. As the subpersonality's resistance begins to melt, you may notice muscles relaxing that even the best massage or physical therapist could not have loosened.

7. After you have taken several of your subpersonalities for a walk in the sunlight, bring all of them to your Temple of Light. Begin by imagining that they are sitting around you in a circle. Ask them to give you their pledge of commitment

and loyalty to your vision. Keep asking until you can hear unanimous agreement. Then imagine that all of your subpersonalities are joining hands, resonating with you. Feel your full power as they commit to the vision of your highest possible future. Touch each member of your orchestra of subpersonalities with the brightest, purest truth you can. Stand and bask in an experience of oneness, a grand unity between all of your subpersonalities and your soul.

All of your subpersonalities will be changed in some way after this meeting in your temple. Celebrate the beginning of a new relationship with these parts of yourself, which up until now may have had control of a good portion of your energy.

Chapter 10

Dissolving Fears With Trust

No one can avoid the experience of suffering on this planet. The effort to escape suffering, the tremendous resistance to pain, actually increases pain. It can cause you to look for the easy way out, which adds delay to facing and handling true responsibilities. When you simply face the *fear* of pain, you may notice that your secret fantasies of the worst were far more painful (and dramatic) than the event or circumstance itself. Most of the time these fears are so outrageous they may later cause you to smile or laugh when you think of them.

Some personality friction is natural, even among spiritual people. The more the personality attempts to handle a disagreement, the stickier it can become. Efforts to defend one's position easily turn to righteousness on both sides, and the higher purpose in working together is delayed. If you find yourself assigning dark motives to those who have hurt you, bring them on your Bridge of Light to absorb the Solar light with you. The touch of the soul on both of you at the same time may reveal how very frightened they are, how many layers of pain lie around their heart, and how profound is their own suffering. This is where healing happens.

If you could erase one annoying emotion that has caused you to suffer, which would it be? Choose one that annoys you rather frequently and examine its roots. The chances are that you will discover some form of fear behind every hurt, resentment, or guilt.

You may have already discovered that your emotions determine your experiences. As you look through the filters of the emotions that are dominant at the time in your energy field, you create the meaning behind the events in your life. Each emotion carries its own pattern and filter. Worry and anxiety, for example, create cloudy filters of grays and murky browns or greens. Lighter emotions give you a clear window to the world, or else they tint it with rose, transparent blue, green, or golden hues.

The Healing Flame of Your Soul

In the center of fear burns the fire of friction. Just as you learned to keep your fingers away from fire, you can also learn to see where emotional fires are burning–and leave them alone. If you discover fear building within your field of energy, you can use the flame of your soul, the cool white Solar fire, to put it out. The Bridge of Light you are building to your soul brings this healing Solar light into your body and purifies it, rinsing away the dense particles that responded to outside fears.

If particles of fear get caught in the tiny filaments of light in your etheric body, you now have the tools to wash them out. The etheric body is the structure that underlies your physical body. Its substance vibrates at a higher rate than physical matter, and it is very sensitive to the fears of those people with whom you are connected. Sometimes you might experience others' fears as a sticky, cobweblike substance in your energy field. The exercise at the end of the chapter shows you how to clear this out.

Another cause of fear is the personality's dread of giving any real power over its life to the soul, even as you are seeking to be infused with soul light. As children, we have all experienced moments of fearing the dark, shrinking back from something that might lurch out. As adults, many people have moments of fearing to move past their familiar path, especially if they can't *see* the light on the higher path.

The human tendency to imagine the worst that never happens creates the most suffering – thus escalating fear through misuse of the creative imagination. Some people energize the very thing they most dread by vividly imagining it happening. Fortunately, by understanding this very human tendency, you can deliberately act in a different way by using your imagination to lift yourself into a vibration that fear does not reach. You may have noticed that while you are in your Temple of Light, fears do not exist. When you are focused on spinning strands of light to soul love, soul joy, soul truth, or soul trust, fears cannot enter. When you bring a friend or teacher to your Bridge of Light and both of you stand there in your luminous Essence Selves, only a sense of deep understanding and love abides.

Your Protective Light

Occasionally, you may be drawn into other people's energy fields that are heavy and dense. They may be polite, saying all the right things, yet you begin to feel depressed, anxious, or fearful for no reason. Your own negative feelings seem out of proportion. No one has consciously intended you any harm, but any stray, dense vibrations in one energy field can provide an entry point for similar vibrations in another. This means that the fears of whomever you are with have found a temporary lodging in your energy field. The antidote is obvious; excuse yourself and in the next few moments spin your Bridge of Light to loving understanding and wait until you feel its protective light around you.

Your work in these times is to deal *only* with negativity from your own psyche. If you sense an emotional upheaval approaching you from outside, let it pass over you without fearing or fighting it. *You are absolutely protected from any outside forces that could harm you when you are in your Temple of Light.* See all negative thoughts that come your way as tiny arrows that are unable to pierce the target and keep glancing off and falling harmlessly to the ground.

As you raise your vibrations to receive from your soul, the familiar fears begin to disappear—fears of making foolish decisions, of losing your path, of hurting others, of not being able to accomplish what you see is possible. Above all, the fear of failing to use your money, your time, your energy, and your mind in the wisest ways changes from self-doubt to the reassurance that you can and will use every asset and skill with greater wisdom. Honestly acknowledge the progress you are making, and your progress speeds up.

Infusing Your Mind With Light

You may have noticed that you do not live according to chronological time; rather you live for a little while in next week, then in last October, then in tonight, then back to ten years ago, and so forth. Once the mind is cultivated by the soul, this kind of time travel can be useful. However, until the conscious mind is under the control of the higher mind and soul, you may be traveling into places that are blocking out the light of your soul and giving you unnecessary pain and suffering.

The mind that has not yet been cultivated by the soul travels into the past – by simply thinking about it – and experiences once again the anguish of that moment, amplifying the fear until adrenaline to help you escape is surging into your bloodstream, with the heart pumping fast and muscles tightening for escape. Blood vessels close up to preserve energy, and all extra functions of the body are interrupted – all this because of mulling over a fearful experience in the past.

Your control of the images you create with your soul will develop steadily. Whatever you put your attention on will grow and flourish; whatever you dismiss as undeserving of your attention will diminish and disappear. So it is with all your fears. You draw them up out of the deep water of your subconscious mind and acknowledge their presence. Then you deliberately build links to the qualities that enrich your life until these are the dominant notes of your life.

Through the power of your higher mind and soul, you are learning to use your mind to cultivate the unseen substance of the etheric plane. It is from this substance (as yet unseen by most people) that good fortune or bad fortune is planted, nourished, and cultivated until it produces its fruit in the material world.

A soul-cultured mind plants thought seeds, nourishes them carefully, and enjoys the bountiful harvest. It knows what is growing and sets the table for the feast. It evolves past the stage of focusing on the past or on other people's lives and getting involved in their personal karma. Your soul-cultured mind can select the seeds to produce something of great value. The power of this mind grows, and follows a path to illumination.

As you bring your mind under the illumination of your soul, you can cooperate with other minds that are planting similar seeds. The community of higher minds—already a reality in the higher dimensions—can then become a community of conscious minds. Miracles of spiritual regeneration can take place as these group seeds planted and nourished together yield a bumper crop, with abundant fruit to share.

Infusing Your Emotions With Light

Each day, soul light flowing through you from your Bridge of Light can create fear-resistant patterns in your energy field and feed your emotions with its finer vibration, color, tone, and rhythm. Gradually, layer upon layer of lighted filaments carrying beautiful colors and sounds take the place of darker ones. Since all who come into your electromagnetic field of energy respond to the note and rhythm that emanate from it, they receive untold blessings when your note is pure and your rhythm is synchronized with the soul.

Here is what happens. As your mind produces thoughts, certain emotions arise in response to each one that match the tone of the thought. Happy or unhappy, optimistic or pessimistic—all of these feelings depend upon the thought that precedes them. The Bridge of Light brings more light into your energy field, and a friction is set up between the new patterns of emotions and the old patterns. This inner friction will be visible on the outside through your relationships to other people, to your work, and most of all to yourself. Alternating between the higher and the lower vibrations, your emotions may seem unstable at first. Yet it is through this process that outmoded patterns can be broken up and reformed. In the process, you may have ups and downs of moods, clear and then fuzzy days, times of effective activities and times of noneffective ones. Pay special attention to the clear spaces— the times of productivity and creativity. Congratulate that part of your being for its good work, and you will multiply these blessings. Remember, all that you give your attention to will grow and flourish.

When you make a commitment to choose a life that is dominated by your Higher Self instead of your personality, you begin to attract people who respect and honor your new path. Your added vibrancy attracts experiences to you that give you many opportunities to use all the light you have brought in. Your best validation, encouragement, and assistance come from the God within, the loving wise Self. Your experiences with others awaken an amazing potential to see a greater truth of who you are.

Becoming Immune to Others' Fears

1. Spend leisure time with friends who have a similar trust in the Spiritual Self and who are working on the path of spiritual growth. They emit a force that supports a trusting love. It is in their aura just as it is in yours, and your group aura creates a very healthful atmosphere.

2. Wear a finely woven cape of light when you are in crowds. After all, you are a weaver in the light. Why not weave a cape of light and wear it to protect you from negative energies? Imagine the weave being so fine that it protects you from dense particles of energy, yet allows finer particles to enter.

Building walls or partitions around yourself for protection is not a good idea. They are far more difficult to dismantle than to build, and it is easy to isolate yourself without realizing it so that no one can approach you. It is far better to risk "catching" someone else's fear than to hide out. A momentary flash of fear is better than a permanent wall that barricades you from true contact with others. You have the tools to handle an invading fear and wash it away. You can become immune to catching people's negative emotions just as you can become immune to catching their colds. As your trust and compassion become stronger than their negativity, their fears and anxieties do not intrude upon your energy field. If fear should find lodging in your mind, you can recognize and dismiss it with a word, as you would a blue jay approaching to steal your food at a picnic.

3. Try this energizing and restoring experience: Find someone whose energy field is so infused with light that you can hear yourself speaking from a deeper level when you are with that person—someone who encourages you to feel expanded, compassionate, wise, joyful, and charged with the enthusiasm to go forward. Spend a few hours with this person and choose a higher purpose to focus on.

4. Look for your soul group on the physical plane. When the substance in a group or individual's heart center is radiating with light, you can recognize that you are finding those with whom you came here to work, those with whom you have worked in other lives, those whose path is similar to yours. This sense of being embraced by love creates a stronger sense of aliveness, and of gratitude for the opportunity to be here on this planet! Many describe this as a sense of being forgiven for every mistake, an opportunity to begin with a clean slate, and a confidence that they can do it. What happens is that the personalities are overshadowed by the pure energy of love inherent

in both souls, and the two souls merge for a timeless moment, producing a new note, a new fragrance, and a new color.

Embracing New Opportunities

By cosmic law, no lesson is presented that is beyond your capacity and experience to handle well. Some people are afraid that their soul has created this physical life only to learn painful lessons. They feel trapped and consequently do nothing, hoping to avoid suffering. But they lose a wonderful opportunity. Lessons do not mean punishment; they do not cause a negative experience. In school, there are math lessons, language lessons, and art lessons. Only the fear of not doing well makes one dread these lessons. Place your confidence in your soul's awesome intelligence and begin to anticipate lessons with delight, with an awareness that each experience raises your confidence and diminishes old fears. As you develop the attitude that you are doing a wonderful job considering your lack of experience and the challenge at hand, all learning can be exhilarating.

Fear of making mistakes exists to ensure that you take that pattern of fear and shift it into light *before* making a decision. The concept of mistakes is an illusion. If you had known a better way at the time, you would have used it. Only now, looking back after becoming wiser from experience, can you say that you made a mistake. Repeating the same action again would indeed be a mistake, but no one would do that. Once you really learn that it does not work, you naturally try a wiser or more loving way. Repeated experiences are such blessings; they allow you to learn what works and what doesn't work and thus help raise you to the next level. Ideal timing

91

and ideal action come only from experience. Whatever you look back on as a mistake was actually the most expedient way to learn a very important lesson. The greater the mistake seems to be, the more important the lesson, and the more surely you learned it once and for all. Once you understand this, you can lighten up and let go of reminding yourself to do "better" the next time. Simply apologize to your psyche, lighten up, and let yourself smile or laugh at the amazing tricks that you have played on yourself to keep down the buoyant delight of wise love.

Small fears frequently hide behind a seemingly practical "reason" to delay your spiritual work on the Bridge of Light, such as reading the newspaper instead of taking the twenty minutes needed to build your bridge to the soul. Whenever you procrastinate and put off a task, some fear lies behind this. Fear of boredom, of failure, of unending work, of unpleasant discoveries—any fear will do. The solution is to check with different subpersonalities and find out which one you have forgotten to honor your commitment with. Often, you are not building in a reward of play after a project is done, and thus are not getting any cooperation from the side of you that thrives on play. Learning to fulfill your commitments to subpersonalities, even small ones, helps you develop the habit of keeping commitments with your soul and with your soul group.

Transforming Indecision on the Bridge of Light

Sometimes you will face choices between two options and feel unsure which course to take. For example, if there are two jobs open, both in the field you desire, and it is very important that you take the one in which you would be most effective in serving, how would you make the choice? After considering the people you would be working with, their expectations, your own abilities, and your own creative desires, what next? Your decision will be much clearer if you uncover any fears by asking yourself, "If there were some anxiety that was veiling my clear vision, what would it be?" If you look at choices this way, many fears can be handled by your rational mind. Fears are nearly always irrational and quickly subside once your rational mind has the opportunity to deal with them. Let your rational mind act as a kindly parent and reveal the true opportunities in the choice you are about to make.

Next, seek a direct knowing by entering your Temple of Light. Fears remain outside the door of the temple, reluctant to enter such a glowing, radiant place. Once you are inside, you can tune your spiritual antennae to intuition and sense which job offer stands in the greater light. Intuition works through symbols, and one picture can give you more information than a thousand words. This process can work to help you resolve any situation that presents you with two or more distinct choices.

Building Trust to Take You Through Mass Fear or Panic

There are times you can benefit from taking refuge in your Temple of Light until a wave of fear created by mass anxiety passes over. Panic arises in waves as astral plane storms affect people's emotions. When these waves hit, many people veer off course, as a flock of birds veers when the lead bird decides there is danger ahead. The time is approaching rapidly when your trust must be placed in your soul's guidance and in your own common sense and consciously refuse to react to mass anxiety about the future of this planet and its people.

Both fear and trust are powerful forces; they create whatever they are focused upon. Fear in the unconscious mind creates the belief that the end of the civilized world is coming. Major cataclysms are not destined to happen to our planet, but mass fear and mistrust can build dark areas in the etheric web around the planet and cause a dissonant vibration. Trust adds a bright electric blue to strengthen this protective web of light and enhance its resonance throughout the Universe.

If you find yourself caught in a crosscurrent of fear or panic, remember that many great intelligences and beings of light from outside this planet are focusing light upon the Earth at this pivotal point of human transformation. They are sending light into the minds of all humanity and love into the hearts of all humanity. Remember this in case of fear, and shake off any residue of fear from your aura, as a shaggy dog shakes water from its coat. Then rinse your aura with a shower of light—as described in the next exercise.

If you clear fear out of your energy field daily, you can dissolve the negative emotions that the fear gives birth to. By taking a shower each day, you wash off the physical dust and grime you've accumulated; by washing off all of the particles of fear in your energy field, you benefit your whole being.

Rinsing Your Aura With a Shower of Light

If doubts or fears arise, this process can help you immediately. Any imbalance in the body, emotions, or mind sends a signal to the brain. If you heed the signal, you can restore inner harmony and trust very quickly. A shower of light does for the psychic body what a shower of fresh water does for the physical body. It washes away the dust and grime of frustrations that have crossed your energy field. After a day out in the world, where you may come into contact with psychic turmoil, rinsing your psyche off with a shower of light restores and rejuvenates your energy. It prevents the lodging of denser material in your aura. It takes only five minutes or less.

1. Imagine a ray of light that emanates directly from your soul above your head. Let it form a spray of light, like a shower. Imagine liquid droplets of light falling all over your body and about three feet around it.

2. If you need stronger trust, use blue light. Imagine this liquid light flowing over and through your body. Continue until you feel lighter inside and out.

A financial manager who has several employees in her department began to shower each one with light when they became anxious or edgy. To create the shower of colors, she first made a very strong Bridge of Light to love. Otherwise she couldn't hold the beautiful and transparent colors in her mind clearly. These showers of light worked so well that she began to shower all of the group in her office with light the first thing in the morning to "fluff up their auras." This took only a couple of minutes, and the reward was an atmosphere of cheerfulness and a genuinely cooperative spirit. Soon, sick days dropped dramatically; the members of her department stayed healthy and actually wanted to come to work. Her own workload became noticeably lighter, and she set up her home life in the same way, using showers of light and colors flowing from her Bridge of Light. Her showers of colors play a major part in transforming her personal relationships into positive and joyful experiences.

Chapter 11
Crises and Challenges as Spiritual Doorways

If you could see yourself as the teachers on the inner side see you, you would stand amazed at how far you have come on the path of spiritual transformation. Your courage to open to the reality of the soul's wisdom makes a dramatic change in your field of energy. You are beginning to purify many of the colors in your aura, and each color represents a soul quality that you are developing. These higher qualities are developed as a result of recognizing and meeting the opportunities presented to you as challenges or points of new decisions. They are opportunities presented through crises and challenges.

A crisis does not mean suffering or fear or pain. It means a juncture, a point of change, or a new recognition. When the old and the new collide and come face-to-face, the old no longer fits. You are bringing the old into harmony with the new in any crisis. A big challenge or crisis is the result of seeing a higher vision, of having a clearer mind or new values, of having the ability to put into practice something you have learned from your soul.

Every challenge is a chance to weave another strand of light on your Bridge of Light. Think of such experiences as revealing a new way to perceive, to think, to feel, as an opportunity to choose more light and take original action rather than follow the familiar response. The wisdom that you have already learned was gained from such experiences. Sometimes, the opportunity is to learn to love more than you have ever loved before, to develop a divine understanding or divine patience. Nearly always, a challenging situation holds within its center the gift of the very spiritual attributes that you have most desired. Once you consciously place yourself on the path of spiritual awakening and expansion, every experience can sweep you forward on your path. The more challenging the experience, the more gain is possible.

Challenges are open invitations to make a jump to a higher level. They signal greater responsibility—a sure sign of your progress in spiritual transformation. Remember, challenge does not mean pain; crisis does not mean suffering. Pain and suffering come at moments when the personality is separated from the soul. All that challenges require is a moment of high creativity, implicit trust in your ability to put your ideas into action, and a steady focus on a successful outcome. When you are weaving a new situation with a lighted mind and lighted emotions, you may find it is more like a treasure hunt. You put all the clues together until you discover the treasure that has been hidden underground.

Surrendering to the Soul's Protection

This is a moment of great truth—when the personality surrenders control and reaches to the soul for direction. A great light floods the person's entire being. In the midst of an emergency, for example, the personality recognizes its limits and surrenders its hold to invoke the soul. The soul may bring an angel on the scene to suspend you in time, shifting you into another dimension of reality, until the emergency is handled. The soul and the angel work outside of time. You may remember some emergencies when you acted with such speed and wisdom that it seemed as if "someone" else took over. You may remember that everything moved into slow-motion; there was plenty of time to see what to do. You were, for that brief moment, looking from the eyes of the soul.

The soul doesn't cause a physical crisis. Crises happen when life is out of balance. Even with physical accidents, you may have a strange feeling that a misfortune might happen unless you make a change. Impressions or dreams may show you that you are overstressed and borrowing on next week's energy.

Times of spiritual intervention can take place not only in emergencies involving physical danger; they can also happen when there is a life-changing decision to be made or when there is an intense internal conflict where two sides of your mind are taking opposite sides. Look over your life at some of the crises you have handled—physical, emotional, and mental ones. Notice how each challenge or crisis has given you the experience and understanding you needed to master some quality that was very important to your spiritual growth. Challenges you face today and handle from your Bridge of Light will not seem like challenges if they appear again. Once you add the skill of a more illumined mind to handle a conflict, that situation is not likely to happen again. You will no longer have any fear around it, and therefore you will not tend to draw it to your life again. If your soul has arranged it in response to your desire to grow spiritually, your soul will have no reason to set it up once you have gained all that it has to offer.

Friction is the path of the personality; it is an early warning sign to begin gathering greater love or wisdom into your energy field. All friction in life requires bringing in a new quality that heals with its finer vibration. If you face a new situation that requires greater resources of knowledge or compassion than you have, build your Bridge of Light to the qualities that you need. Then immerse yourself in them until your mind and emotions are infused with these qualities.

Freeing Your Mind and Emotions for Their True Work

As you may have observed, the same event can trigger a crisis in one person while another person shrugs or laughs it off. A crisis is determined not so much by the event itself, but by the interpretation of the event. Here is a way to become the one who smiles or laughs rather than the one who cries at unexpected events.

As soon as something happens that would ordinarily disturb your equanimity, stop and create several outrageously positive interpretations of its meaning. Let each interpretation become more outrageous. How does the event prove that you are protected, that your requests are heard and being answered? What wonderful quality is this event offering to you? How many years have you saved because of learning so quickly what would take most people a whole lifetime to learn—years that give you the strength, courage, and freedom to make a difference in the world? Invite a friend with a good imagination to play with you, and you will soon see that these playful interpretations of the real meaning behind the event could well be the real truth, while the fearful interpretation had nothing to do with the truth.

At some time, you have probably been challenged with a crisis that seemed to be coming entirely from the outside. Yet it was your desire to purify your life and eliminate an old pattern that drew that particular crisis to you. It might have been a crisis of physical health, emotional trauma, or a mental clash of beliefs. For example, if you discover that you are bringing out the worst in someone while someone else is bringing out the best in that person, examine where the tiny seed of the same pattern you bring out lies within your own energy field. Most probably there is just enough to draw out a similar pattern in the other person.

Solving Problems in a Higher Light

As you contact higher vibrations of light, all challenges you face save you from a humdrum life of simply coasting along year after year, meeting the same problems without rising high enough to ever solve them. Remember, problems can only be solved in a higher light than the one in which they were created.

In the past age, the big jolts that shook up people's automatic habits came only rarely. When these inner earthquakes were over, people could relax and expect to live peacefully for many years. This meant that little progress was made in one lifetime. Now, as waves of the finer frequency of light come into the planet, waves of new awareness are more frequent. They remind you to reach higher; they force you to explore greater possibilities and to use your life energy wisely and well.

Any challenge that seems too hard to handle actually comes only after your tacit agreement that you now have the strength and knowledge to handle it. Remember, a break-through in an unproductive situation frees up time for productive activities. An explosion of temper clears the air for real communication and understanding. Don't criticize yourself when things aren't running smoothly. Give thanks for the opportunity to polish those facets of yourself so they can reflect the light and color of your soul.

The more you send help to all souls who are learning with you, the more help you can accept from your own illumined Essence Self. Give a silent blessing to everyone over the world who is handling the same challenge as you—and there are many. See them drawing from their souls an inner strength, wisdom, and compassion they didn't know they had. Send the love of your soul and the light of your mind to them.

Facing a Crisis

A crisis point of choice rarely appears suddenly. It builds with many checkpoints to reveal where the situation is leading. Watch for these checkpoints, and meet the situation there. The farther ahead you see a problem building, the less energy and time are involved in handling it. Sometimes you can take wise action before stormy waves build up on the emotional level and handle it from the mental level. For example, if you find your career empty and want to change it for a career closer to your heart, you can learn the skills needed, make connections, and prepare the path for change, perhaps with an interim job to make the transition.

As your link with your soul becomes strong and clear,

it is possible to see so much at once that you feel mentally overwhelmed. One woman we assisted was making such rapid spiritual shifts that she felt she had no solid ground to stand on and that what she had achieved so far in life was meaningless, a complete waste of her life. Yet, two years later she had quit her high-pressure executive job and started a small flower shop, the work that was closest to her heart. Her successful transition was easier because of all the practical management skills she had learned in her previous jobs.

If you are experiencing a sense of being overwhelmed, you may want someone to tell you what to do. Unfortunately, others cannot judge which decision is the wisest for you. They can tell you about their own experience; they can help you remain calm and clear while you explore all possibilities. But the wisdom you need lies within the center of your soul and can best be revealed from the stillness of your Temple of Light. As a result of the deep search and the decision made in a clear light, you gain a gentler spirit, filled with compassion, understanding, and humility. These gradually become part of your natural response in every situation.

Receiving Assistance From Illumined Souls

Whenever you are experiencing this overwhelmed feeling, first, go into your Temple of Light and release all feelings of panic and anxiety. Rise into the vibration of your soul and consciously link with all the illumined souls and masters who are guiding humanity with great wisdom and compassion. Imagine your soul linking with them as a group, offering all that they have and all that they know. Feel the strength of this group. Even though you have no physical contact with them, the soul contact is profoundly healing, giving you an immediate lift of spirit. There are always those on the inner planes who are working with very high frequencies of Solar light and distributing this light and love to the minds and hearts of all who can receive it. When you connect telepathically with this group of advanced souls and masters who are ceaselessly working to help humanity and the planet, a wonderful energy sweeps through your heart center and higher mind. You feel healed and rebalanced, supported and loved. Embraced in this womb of wisdom and love, you can see the deeper issues before you and understand what is needed for you to move forward on the path of illumination.

You may strongly benefit from linking with this group every day. Add the light of your soul to the group soul and drink in the pulsating rhythm of the energy here. You may sense the power of the grid work of the group and tap into a pool of knowledge created by the combined light of this group. We invite you to open to receive from this group of planetary servers.

Taking the Practical Steps

The practical steps that you take after deep reflection are possible only after you have made a true commitment to the higher path of the soul. Whether you consciously realize the life-changing choice you have made or whether it takes place in your higher mind outside of your conscious awareness, changes for the better will begin to happen in your outer physical life. Each one tests your commitment, and each one brings a new blessing of vision, freedom from the pull of the past, and a brighter spirit!

A trained counselor can sometimes prove helpful, especially if he or she has a strong spiritual focus. Or you may benefit from talking with a wise and loving friend. Be sure this is someone who knows how to listen well, without giving advice too quickly, and someone who can help you hold a focus on the real issues you are working with.

Another possibility is to find a local meditation group that is open to guests. This may prove a route to connecting with groups or individuals who may have been through what you are facing. Ask your metaphysical bookstore manager to suggest books to read. Often a book may offer the best outside help because it stimulates the answers to come from within, whereas untrained people have a tendency to give you answers that would work best for themselves. Search for books that have an aura of light around them. This energy is more powerful than words alone.

Opening the Space for a Richer Life

Each crisis reflects some area of life that is being healed and restructured. These gains are much easier to see after your life is calm and normal again. If the value of a crisis is not clear, ask for insights and insights will come. Often the loss of money, the loss of a job, or the loss of a relationship can offer a new level of freedom and self-awareness that wasn't there before. Any loss on the material plane creates the space to draw to yourself something that is far more valuable to your spiritual transformation than what was lost. Pain arises from the difficulty of the personality to understand this principle. Any suffering is in proportion to your fantasy of how wonderful life would have been if the loss hadn't happened.

Make a fantasy of a different kind, which will of course be just as likely to be true, and watch your pain turn to relief.

You are learning how to discriminate beliefs which have a higher grade of substance in their essence from those which do not. Illusions begin to look ephemeral, more like a temporary apparition, less solid and real. Just as the Earth looks flat when you stand on a prairie, and yet is obviously round when you are flying high above it, many beliefs that you have accepted will shift as a higher truth embraces them. Use humor when you recognize another illusion that has kept your mind in a prison. Letting go is much easier with an inner smile.

Beliefs left over from childhood can be shaken loose through the new light, including beliefs of inferiority, discouragement, or unworthiness. Imagine that a space is being cleared on the landing field of your mind, opening the way for creative ideas that are flying around you to make a smooth landing. Thoughts may start flowing to you when you least expect them—in the midst of a lively discussion or in the silence of your dreams. These thoughts may be practical, concerning a new place to live, or a way to connect with a group on a similar path of discovery, or they may be formless, gathering energy before reaching the physical plane to be manifested.

If your mind should start going in circles without really getting anywhere when you are trying to make an important decision, give yourself a well-deserved rest. Cleaning out the garage or weeding the garden may seem like a funny opening for the understanding you are looking for, but often the best ideas can come through when the body is engaged and the mind is at ease. Try using everything as a metaphor. Dispose of an empty can of old paint from the garage and feel your spirit lift as if you were throwing out an old belief that doesn't enrich your life. Or pull up an overgrown weed and feel the relief as you lift it out roots and all.

Handling crises and challenges can be exhilarating—a bit like paddling a kayak. The first skill one learns is how to roll the kayak. Kayakers purposely turn their tiny boats over and then roll them all the way around until they turn upright again, all while they remain seated. Once they master their rollover recovery in a calm lake, they have a better idea of how to handle themselves when they run into the big waves.

If you lose your temper or become irritable with your mate, impatient with your child, or resentful toward your boss, think of this as a rollover that allows you to practice bringing yourself upright again. Even though you may still be in the middle of white water as your balance is regained, you can simply fasten your eyes on where you are going and paddle vigorously until the water is calm and clear.

If, on certain days, you feel as if you are going backward instead of forward, stop and visualize yourself "riding light in the saddle," with a renewed sense of humor, able to see how sure your feet are becoming on your Bridge of Light. Do this as if your life depended on it. Then spend three or four minutes bringing all those to your bridge who most need help to clear their future for experiences of true fulfillment and happiness. Regardless of how unworthy you may feel at the moment, you are absolutely capable of holding someone else in the light and sensing the difference it makes as light flows into that person's soul. No matter how discouraged you are, your soul is not in the least involved; it can do its work at any moment when you are willing to direct its light through you and outward into the world. No matter how little love you may feel that you have to offer on such days, your soul is infinitely rich with an intelligent love that literally heals whatever it touches. It stands ready to burn away the dross and reveal only the gold in any situation – when you ask it do so.

There are physical crises, emotional crises, mental crises, and spiritual crises. And you can learn to recognize the presented opportunity in each one without fear or anguish, but confident of a successful outcome with your tools of light.

Physical Crises: An Invitation for Deep Healing

If you are ill, weakened, or physically handicapped in any way, you can look on this as a motivator to accelerate your spiritual transformation. The illness is a constant reminder to stay focused, to build in the thoughts, emotions, and the spiritual flow that rebuild your cells. As you heal your body and wash toxins out of your body, you are also washing them out of your entire energy field. You can identify debris that has collected within your life and wash it away at the same time. With the additional light of the soul, you can regenerate and heal more than your body; you can bring in the deep healing of your soul. At the end of the crisis, you can see how to build a life that is superior to the one you had as well as a body that is superior to the one you had. Book II of this series, *Healing With Light,* gives you a whole system to heal and regenerate your body with light.

Emotional Crises: Clearing the Way for True Joy

Every lively negative emotion you experience – from hurt to anger, rage, or guilt – calls attention to a part of the personality that is asking for an even stronger connection to the light. Sometimes crying releases the inner pressure. At other times, humor helps even more as you see the common human frailties of all personalities. Many emotional challenges can be shifted on the Bridge of Light to love. Be willing to see and acknowledge any personality tendencies that set up a crisis on the emotional plane, such as being demanding, controlling, impatient, self-indulgent, irresponsible, or over-sensitive to hurt. You can handle these by training your mind to take charge of your emotions.

If negative emotions are pushed back and you feel pressure building into a depression, spin a Bridge of Light to lightness and humor. After you are standing on the bridge to humor, ask: If there were a way to feel lighter now, what would it be? Nearly always, some idea will come to you. Next, deliberately choose an activity that allows you to experience the emotions you do enjoy. For example, you can contact several people who are important to you and tell them so. Or call some friends and tell them how much you appreciate who they are. Such activities release you from a wave of negative energy that has washed over you so that you can ride the waves of positive energies that are rolling in so powerfully now.

Mental Crises: Choosing the Lighted Way

A mental crisis begins when there is a clash of two strong beliefs that are in direct opposition to each other. As you contact inspiration on your Bridge of Light, old beliefs may conflict with new ones. For example, you may believe that your life will not be complete unless you have children and yet you see an opportunity to offer some valuable work in education for thousands of children that would require your full time without children of your own. You believe that your money should be used to support the new global changes and yet also feel compelled to use it for yourself. Or you may believe that marriage should last forever and yet recognize that your relationship is empty because both of you have taken entirely different paths in life. These are crises that require you to bring a greater light into your mind – the light of illumination – and look into the future to see the best choice.

A Bridge of Light to wisdom and clarity illumines your mind to choose the lighted way. The illumined mind can see with such clarity that it can make a decision based upon a higher truth. You can bring this illumination to your mind by calling in a Bridge of Light to clarity and to wisdom. The energy of these two soul qualities will fill your mind with the insights and the understanding that it needs when such challenges and crises arise.

Spiritual Crises: A Doorway to Initiation

A spiritual crisis is a crossroads for the soul that creates such waves of change that every part of you is affected – body, mind, and emotions. When you face a soul crisis directly, a new consciousness is born. This crisis is not over quickly; it calls for deep reflection, for life-changing decisions, and a clear commitment from the most profound depths of your being. The choice you make will affect the rest of your life.

When you face a spiritual crisis, a very strong bridge between the personality and soul is essential. This bridge becomes the saving grace by providing some understanding of what is happening and assisting you to use all the knowledge, inner strength, and patience that you can invoke.

If you find yourself facing a spiritual crisis, it may feel as if winds are whipping around you, causing you to lose your sense of direction and balance. The outer world goes on as before, but if you are in the midst of a soul crisis you can feel utterly bereft, isolated, confused, or helpless. Your rational mind cannot handle this kind of crisis by itself. You simply know that something terribly important is missing in your life and that you must find it, whatever the cost.

Such a crisis is a great blessing, sweeping out the energy that is unsuited for the higher path and opening the door of new opportunity that could not be opened otherwise. It is a preparation for a higher initiation and reaches into the core of the being, deeply affecting your future. Out of this crisis, you emerge into an expanded state of being and gradually bring your life into alignment with the new rhythm and direction of the soul.

It may seem as if a crisis of this kind is being caused by some situation over which you have no control—that the world is doing it to you. But these crises only happen when you have made the inner commitment to see them through, to handle whatever is standing in the way of your ascending to a higher dimension. It may seem as if some commitment you made long ago is only now coming to light, to be remembered and acted upon. The crisis offers you the opportunity to clear every obstruction to your transformation. Illusions that confused your mind begin to clear and, behold, a new life becomes possible!

How you restructure your life after a spiritual crisis is very important. In the expanded state of awareness that follows a true spiritual crisis, you are offered greater world service, clearer seeing into the future, the healing power of spiritual love, greater knowledge of the spiritual life, and a closer contact with the master who is guiding you.

Here are some warning signs to help you recognize, move through, and integrate your life in a spiritual crisis.

- A deep discontent begins; you feel dissatisfied with your whole life, not just one small part of it, even though you have achieved most of what you set out to do.
- You know that something very, very important is missing, and you cannot push that knowledge out of your head regardless of the distractions and entertainments that you set up for yourself.
- You lose the keen focus of your rational mind that has always served you well before. You realize that it cannot get you out of this serious dilemma. You may even contemplate the idea of ending your life.
- You begin to see the many layers of your personality that are built over the soul and to work your way through them as you contemplate very deeply what to do.

Moving Through a Spiritual Crisis

1. Decide to face your worst fears—which may include fears that you have no soul or spirit, and that there is no God. Or your worst fear may be that you are a complete and utter failure in life and there is no point in continuing.

2. Write a letter to your soul, stating your fears and your suffering. Ask for help.

3. In a few days, assume the role of your soul and let it answer the letter from your personality. You will be amazed

112

at the wisdom that flows into your mind as you write. Many of your most searching questions will be answered clearly, in a straightforward manner. The truth revealed to you will be obvious.

4. Continue to handle your life on the material plane as best you can. During such a crisis, you are in no position to make wise choices. This you do as the intensity lessens and you are able to integrate the light that has poured into you and created this spiritual crisis. Keep your job, your family, your home as they are during the crisis. If you escape from any true responsibilities, you must return and complete what you did not finish; it is more efficient to handle them now. Give yourself three years to put your new life together.

5. Many people will have no idea that you are going through a crisis. If you have spiritual friends, ask them to meditate and surround you with light. Their loving prayers will lift and encourage you.

6. Turn to the Masters of Life who guide humanity, even if you have doubts that they really exist. Or turn to your guardian angel. You will receive help.

7. Keep your body well. Get exercise, eat healthy food, and get enough sleep.

8. Be patient with the process and with yourself. Be kind to the people closest to you even if you don't feel like it. You need their love more than ever, and all love is healing.

9. Know that this spiritual crisis is temporary; it will not last one minute longer than it takes to break up the crystallization that has taken place in your mind and body. It is here as a gift from your soul to remove everything that belongs to the you who existed before a great inflow of light came to you. Every thought and belief, every emotion, every physical vibration that prevented you from taking your next step in your spiritual transformation will leave as a result of this crisis.

Chapter 12
Letting Go With Love

The next step in building a new life is to attract experiences on the physical plane to put all this light into. Your work is to turn this highly refined vibrating energy into practical knowledge and power—and make it yours. Only after you have tested new knowledge in the physical world can your soul store it as a permanent part of your being. In this chapter, you will learn how to create the space for positive new experiences by releasing the old ones with love.

Rather than trying to understand why you have negative thoughts and emotions, simply choose the thoughts and emotions you do want and begin to build these into your everyday life and your relationships. Fortunately, no experiences in your life are wasted energy. Your most delightful experiences build your new life, and your least delightful experiences build your new life. Both are used to nourish your spiritual life when your intention is to do so. Whether experiences feel good or bad, happy or unhappy, your soul stores them as wisdom. The soul builds new colors into its light body through your experiences regardless of the emotional reactions you have. Anxiety and worry do, however, prevent your soul from being able to give you the true delight of living, loving, and learning. For example, if you worry about growing old or sick, being poor or lonely, these feelings, even if they are unconscious, clutter your energy field and block your soul from a strong connection with you.

You are not at the mercy of negative emotional reactions to any situation. You can build a new emotional response by observing a personality reaction that you don't like and replacing it with a more refined and useful response. The old emotion is replaced with an equal volume of lighted energy. Gradually, each part of you that formerly got caught in a web of emotional intrigue is no longer seduced by fear or emotional drama. These parts of your life are filled with the regenerating power of your soul, giving you a steady flow of emotional energy that allows you to love life and to receive clear images from your soul.

You are also not at the mercy of your thoughts about a situation. No dread of the future or misfortune of the past is as great as the power of your soul to heal. You can raise your consciousness to soul wisdom and then look down at any situation that has caused a negative reaction. If you have a patient and positive expectation, a new outlook will nearly always come to you. If you had a sense of helplessness about making that situation work, the helplessness tends to dissolve as new ideas emerge. Remember, all situations can be handled from the awareness that is at least one level higher than the one in which they were created.

The personality loves in order to be loved. Thus, it gets caught up in false obligations, trying to please, to be liked, and to make people be happy. For example, one person in our seminars had a belief that he had to hold everyone up around him. He carried a burden that tired him unnecessarily and that actually weakened the people closest to him; they began to depend on him for their well-being and to blame him if they didn't receive his energy. They could not learn to observe their own thoughts and discover the power of their own Bridge of Light. As he began to create a soul-infused personality, he built a fine discernment; he knew when to assist someone on the physical plane and when to respect that person's rhythm of learning and growing.

Loving as the Soul

The soul loves, but it loves without the human tendency to try to change others; it sees without feeling the need to pressure others to be happy. It doesn't take over other people's struggle and try to loosen all their emotional bindings for them; it does encourage them as they work out their problems. The soul is not self-conscious as the personality is. It is group conscious – aware of its connection and work with other souls. The soul does not know fear – or any other negative emotion. It is free from desire. It loves because it *is* love. Its light body is built of the essence of love.

The soul-infused personality holds a clear vision of others' success and rejoices as they succeed. You build this wise personality by connecting with your true Self moment to moment, aware of yourself as a soul. Your understanding of who you are and where you are going as a soul keeps shifting to a larger picture as new light and knowledge seep into your mind and emotions. Your mind becomes wise in inspired ideas that are on a higher vibratory level than where you are living. Soon, it can retain the original thought form sent by your soul; this gives you the courage to tell the truth as you see it today, and then to re-tell it as you see it next year. If you embrace new ideals of truth as they are revealed to you, you open to your highest expansion.

117

You can let your soul speak through you. This deep communication has integrity; it offers an honest appraisal of new possibilities that only the soul can initiate, free from any pretense or fear.

Letting Your Soul Speak

1. From your Temple of Light, let your soul speak through you. Ask that the cosmic gates of your soul open and release wisdom that has long been encoded within your own heart so you may know more of who you are and sense the incredible light you are within your own being.

2. Issue an invitation to your soul to infuse your mind with its joy, love, and intelligence. Absorb this light into your mind and emotions by an act of will. Write what you sense your soul would say if it had a voice. Include the qualities and inspirations that your soul is bringing to your personality to replace unlighted emotions and thoughts.

3. Write a few ideas on the activities that your soul might begin if it had a body of its own in the physical world. Use the ideas that are most helpful and that allow you to be temperate yet dynamic, ageless with vital energy and strength, focused yet flexible. Ask your soul how to become one who loves, knows, and speaks only from a positive creative intention.

Loving All That You Leave Behind

As you bring light into your life, you may want to leave something behind besides negative emotions and thoughts. If you want to move to a new home, a new neighborhood, a new job, or a new town, you are free to do so. If you first transmute any negative reactions toward whom or what you are leaving behind into positive appreciation, your entrance into the next phase of your life will be easier and much more pleasant. Once you feel positive about where you are now, quite suddenly the path to a new experience will appear that wasn't there before.

If you can truly appreciate whatever you choose to leave before you leave it, sincerely acknowledging the gifts you have received, you open a path of light to your next step. For example, you can transform any relationship to a more positive and creative one when you bring it to your Bridge of Light. One woman wanted to leave her marriage; she had collected many reasons for this decision, and most of them placed the blame on her husband. Realizing that she wanted to surrender her collection of reasons to the wisdom of her soul, she met her husband on a Bridge of Light, not as a personality but as a soul. She didn't try to communicate a message; she just stood there with his shining Essence Self on her bridge. She soon realized how many ways she had hurt him, and she acknowledged this to him on the bridge. Gradually, their relationship became much more harmonious; they could speak to each other honestly without fear. They soon realized that they had successfully completed their purpose together and that now their paths were different; each wanted to pursue a different path, yet was afraid of hurting the other one. Because they had created a positive way of relating, they were able to part without guilt or blame and then go forward to create new lives of happiness and creativity.

As you move into a soul-centered life, a deeper love can emerge for your family and friends. You may think that it is your friends who are changing–and they are–but you are changing as well. If you can resist the temptation to throw someone out of your life to get rid of friction, ending a rela-

119

tionship may be the best move only *after* you have harmonized the inner conflict between your personality and soul that comes up when you are on a path of light. Sometimes you can change the way you relate to another person and create good rapport and support by the change of form alone. For example, if you are usually in control of the conversation, you can divide the time more equally for each person to direct the conversation. You can agree on a higher purpose for each meeting and stay with that purpose. If you find yourself sliding into resentment toward anyone, rather than place the blame on her or him, meet with the Essence Self of that person on your Bridge of Light three or four times. Choose a different soul destination each time, and then observe spontaneous changes in the way you relate to each other.

All who are touched with love when your personality is still glowing from the Bridge of Light will receive a gift. Let your love reach many people and many groups. The more light you bring in, the more places you need to put it. Even one genuine act of loving-kindness may make a greater difference in another person's life (and your own) than a multitude of polite gestures that lack the power of the soul to transform.

Opening Gates to Your New Destination

The soul is the essence energy behind all harmony. Before you leave anything or anyone, find something to give of true value. If you can find a way to offer love right where you are now, the gates swing open to your new destination, and you won't need to try to jump over or crawl under them. When you give from the heart, others receive, and when they receive from you, that part of your life becomes a wonderful adventure.

Imbued with the love of the soul, if you once hated your town, you can now appreciate its attributes. If you felt you didn't belong, you can now realize that you do. Even though you may say good-bye anyway, you can leave a trail of lighted love behind you, a most useful way to move forward in your spiritual life.

When you leave someone or something in a positive state of appreciation and goodwill, you are no longer bound by a negative reaction. You will not walk into dissatisfaction at the next place you go. Instead, you can walk into a new place, recognize its limitations, and appreciate it all the same. One woman hated the little town she and her husband had moved to and asked for her soul to help them get out. After many requests, she finally received a clear understanding: "You are free to leave when you establish your roots here." Exactly ten years later, she realized that she had learned to love the town and all of the people in it. Three days after she had said to herself, "I never want to leave this town; I love it here," her husband decided to move his business to a new town. She was miserable in the new city and began to plead with her soul for a change when she suddenly remembered the path that led to changing towns and settled down to learn to love the new town. Several years later, she realized she loved that town as much as the first one, and, as you might expect, they moved within a month to a new town. This time she decided to enjoy her new hometown from the very first day she arrived.

A mother of three small children wanted to do something that really made a difference in the world. She yearned to help the poor people in developing countries and asked her soul for guidance in becoming a true server for the planet. Her yearning was creating an inner dissatisfaction and some irritability and impatience. The reply she received (as soon as she could get still enough within to listen) was very clear: "We have sent you three highly evolved souls; you have been chosen to be their guide and teacher, and this work is much more important than anything else you can do anywhere in the world." She immediately saw the truth of this revelation and recognized that her role as a mother was a special privilege. She began to have a wonderful time teaching and guiding these three shining souls and now considers her role as a mother to be the most life-changing and fulfilling work she has done.

Perhaps you also want to make a change that might suppress your soul's true work because of a negative reaction about where you are now. Listen very carefully and patiently within your Temple of Light. The answer will come, and when you can put the message it carries into words, you may feel a renewed dedication to complete whatever you have begun. When you know a job or a relationship is truly on your path, there is a deep sense of fulfillment as you engage in it. When it is over and you look back on it, you may recognize that it was one of the most important phases of your life and that you actually gained far more from the experience than you ever imagined possible at the time. If the responsibility that is holding you down is not truly yours, if it is a false obligation, you will realize from your Temple of Light that you can shift out of it gracefully and move on to another adventure.

Meeting as Essence Selves Before Parting

In this guided journey, you have an opportunity to meet a friend as a soul with no personality involvement.

1. Go into your Temple of Light and sit in front of the white fire in the center until you feel the presence of your soul.

2. Bring the person whom you are leaving or thinking of leaving. Forget about any personality frictions, differences in status, or any characteristics of control or selfishness of the personality. You will be meeting as two souls, free from all personality anxiety and worry.

3. Look in the eyes of this person sitting with you in the Temple of Light. Go in through the eyes until you sense the soul and follow a line of light into the very center point of this soul. Here, you can find the presence of the soul as a living energy that carries great love.

4. Holding your focus as a soul, alternate between the soul in front of you and yourself as a soul. You may spend many cosmic hours here learning from each other, sharing and contemplating, and finally returning with a very deep sense of fulfillment—of being accepted, of being loved and understood. And you may discover that only a few minutes of clock time have actually passed. Time does not control the higher planes. Transformation can happen in the wink of the second hand on a clock.

5. When you complete this communication, let the friend leave your Temple of Light and note what you learned about yourself as a soul and about your friend as a soul. Each time you repeat this journey, you can reach a deeper level of communication. If you take the time to describe these journeys in your Temple of Light journal, these experiences serve as agents of your spiritual transformation.

Spinning Cords of Good Fortune into Your Future

Look at your life as it now stands and notice how many areas of your life are beginning to reflect your soul's love and wisdom. Acknowledge the small changes that you are making—and the space for a wonderful life begins to move in. For example, every act that is initiated by your soul streams its light into the future, awaiting your approach there so it may give its gift to you. Whatever you give from the heart without any sense of control or demand comes back to you increased many times over. You begin to understand how the soul light that was given out of compassion or love many years ago has projected itself as a line of light and formed the line of an arc above you and extended itself in the future. At a specific point in your future, the arc gracefully drops and awaits you as an experience of bliss or good fortune.

This is why forgiveness represents such an opportunity. When you feel anger, resentment, hurt, or jealousy toward anyone, you are entangling yourself with that person, and the two of you are bound together like two kittens tangled up in a ball of string. The person with whom you are thus entangled (or a copy of him or her) will reappear in your future until you release the cords that bind you. This is also true of neighborhoods, towns, and countries.

Here is a very simple and effective journey in your temple to release your life from any dense cords from the past arching over and into your future. You are thus eliminating experiences that will not bring happiness or fulfillment and that serve no purpose in being repeated.

Transforming an Experience

1. Go to your Temple of Light; sit in front of the flame of your soul, and bring in every quality that you have built a Bridge of Light to so far—joy, truth, trust, confidence, courage,

love, understanding, harmony, wisdom, and more. Bring all of these soul qualities in a circle around you.

2. Go back in time to an event that feels toxic in some way, such as bringing a bitter taste when you think of it, a queasy feeling in the pit of your stomach, or a headache. Choose an experience where you participated in some way. Bring it to your Temple of Light and place it opposite you with the flame of your soul between you.

3. Locate the hope you felt as you went into it, the hope that you could produce a happy outcome. Find the moment when you realized that you simply did not have the wisdom or the love to make the situation work. You recognized that you did not yet have all the soul qualities needed to generate a good outcome.

4. Decide which qualities would have transformed the situation from one of pain to one of creative energy. Bring these qualities from your circle, one at a time, directly over the event. Stack one on the other, each time doubling the light that is generated into the experience. Observe any shifts in this experience as the Solar light permeates the situation and all of the qualities are shining directly over the experience.

5. Bring the experience into the flame of your soul. Watch it melt until only the essence substance within it remains. This could be a tiny nugget of gold, a small pearl, or a living thing, such as a white butterfly emerging.

Chapter 13

Staying Sane and Still Expanding

You who are reading this book are not likely to fit into the mold for "normal" in the eyes of the general public. *Normal* simply means "average." As you attract and integrate the new frequencies of light, you are on the leading edge of consciousness rather than in the middle. As more and more people recognize the light of the Higher Self or soul as the true source of life, these beliefs will become the norm and those who lag behind will be seen as the young souls. An acceptance of the authentic, powerful stages of human development beyond the personality will come to be expected. There are growing numbers of you, and many more are poised to break through and begin to use the power of their creative imagination with the soul. It will take only a small minority of the thinking minds working with spiritual light to open the path of light for the majority and to furnish a grid work of light that supports a planet of true peace and goodwill.

The process of enlightenment requires a well-integrated personality as a base for the Higher Self's guidance. The light flowing into your mind can stimulate any personality tendency, such as a sense of superiority or inferiority, or emotions of sadness, loneliness, grief, or anger. If a major adjustment is suddenly demanded of your personality, an integration of soul qualities can enable you to make it with grace. These graceful adjustments to changes, even to friends' doubts about your sanity, can be handled with the tools of light you are mastering in each chapter.

Many people are simply afraid to experience a fuller revelation of who they are at this time, and their fear is projected onto you as a concern about your sanity. When you realize how they are feeling, your own compassion and caring can come to the surface. Instead of feeling bad about any judgments they might have about your beliefs, you can simply send them a silent blessing and be on your way.

The quicker you recognize someone's "concern" about you, the easier it is to handle. You may find that some people think there is something wrong with your beliefs. You may have difficulty convincing your own family or partner that you are not going off the deep end.

One woman's intense interest in meditation and metaphysical knowledge disturbed her family so much that she agreed to take all the psychological tests available to reassure them that she was balanced and quite sane. She spent days answering hundreds of questions, drawing pictures, telling stories, and projecting meaning onto inkblots with the psychologist. The results of the tests showed that she was extraordinarily bright, creative, and well integrated mentally and emotionally. Everyone relaxed, and she continued to study and meditate, with an occasional wink to remind her father that she was absolutely normal, even if she was on the high end of normal.

Your personality is working diligently to integrate new circuits of reality. If other people seem to cause disruptions or confusion, recognize them as a valuable part of your expansion in consciousness. Every insight or new understanding gained in meditation must be played out in the world – with your parents, partner, children, boss, and friends. Your integration of soul qualities and your willingness to speak honestly and to listen and accept others just as they are – these are the challenges and victories of a spiritual life.

The most disturbing questioner about your sanity may be a subpersonality in yourself. Meet the part of yourself that questions your sanity or common sense with the same compassionate understanding you extend to your family and friends. If one side thinks you should be more concerned about the material side of life, listen to it and agree that when you consider its viewpoint you can understand how it would feel afraid. (You are using the same logic that you would use with friends who have a similar concern.) The more accepting you can be, the less opposition to your spiritual expansion you will face from within your own self.

Creating New Roles to Play

When the roles you were playing in life are no longer taking you forward, it is time to reflect on the new role you want to play. Enlist the subpersonalities that need some coaching to assist you in your overall picture. By focusing on your creative faculty, you can more quickly move into an effective, purposeful, and powerful life in the new role of an awakened soul.

Be patient with your personality as it assimilates new knowledge. Any knowledge that goes beyond popular beliefs can sometimes cause some part of your personality to feel isolated, especially when there is no proof in the outer world and friends haven't had similar experiences. Remember that self-questioning does not mean that you have a mental or emotional problem. You are simply cleaning your whole field of old habits of thinking in an extremely accelerated manner, and you may not be getting much support in the process.

Developing a supportive atmosphere around you may depend on how many changes the people in your life think you want *them* to make. If you can accept them just as they are without the need for them to be interested in transpersonal awareness, you can ease your path. Remember that they may think spiritual awakening is dangerous, lumping it together with the pseudo-teachings of someone who claims to be a spiritual leader but who lacks wisdom and love. Underneath it, these people care about you. If you can imagine how strong their anxiety must be, you can understand why they are too fearful to investigate any realities beyond the material world.

By being very truthful to yourself and not pretending to be someone else, you will move into true balance and happiness. Speak truthfully to others, but share only what is appropriate. Sometimes it's wise to be silent with others about who you are, but be disarmingly honest with yourself. In this way, you will feel a steady, strong sense of your Higher Self rising from within.

Relationships as an Opportunity

Relationships provide a wonderful opportunity to take friction and conflict and turn them into harmony. Appreciate everyone in your life, for each person you know brings out a different side of your personality. With some friends, you may feel wise and powerful. With others who are very conservative and rigid in their beliefs, you may feel awkward and unable to express your thoughts clearly. In each case, you are responding to people's images as they strike a chord within you.

Notice what annoys you most in others, and you can gain greater insight into a part of yourself that is ready to be recognized and transformed. Your Higher Self can compute the healing vibrations needed and communicate sound and sensible advice to you. Trust it.

Observe several traits in others that most feel attractive and healing to your soul. You will also find these traits within yourself. Take a few minutes to focus on each trait as it exists within your soul and mind. Recall times when you have expressed it. When you acknowledge this trait and connect more closely with it, you make it more available in other areas of your life.

As you make these self-observations, you begin to know yourself, not as a frog or a prince or princess, but as an unfinished work of artistic and spiritual perfection. This is the sane approach to enlightenment: clearly seeing where you are still drawing in new colors and tones and beauty from the soul, and at the same time recognizing the tremendous work that has already been accomplished by the master artist of life, your luminous soul.

Creating Understanding Through Love

The guided journey here is to make a new level of connection with those people who are closest to you–one in which soul love prevails over personality frictions. You will

131

be giving something of great value to them without any desire to get something back. Yet you may discover that you receive from them a special friendship of support and encouragement that was simply not available on the personality level.

1. Go to your Bridge of Light and bring the members of your family and closest friends to the bridge with you.

2. See them in their Essence Selves, shining with different colors on the bridge—ageless, sexless, and without any personality fears or prejudices. See them as shining points of light within a greater light.

3. As your soul, project a great flow of love to each one as a line of light that joins you on the soul plane. Love as you have never loved before. Weave this line of light around each one.

4. Ask the Essence Self of each one to shower its personality self with this love. You may be surprised at the energy that comes back to you as you create this journey on your Bridge of Light. You are giving the quality of love that everyone yearns for and is most benefited by receiving. After these journeys, you may find that the group you have brought to your bridge becomes warmer and more at peace with you than ever before.

Part Three

Creating Your
Highest Possible Future

About Part Three

Now you are ready to begin to create your most purposeful and joyous future. You will deliberately be choosing to live by the authority of your own soul, and you will be aware of and responsible for the results of these choices. The inner strength that you gain from freely choosing your life prepares you for finding the field of service that is most attractive to you. You will then learn ways to change your future by changing your past and ways to energize your physical body. Next, you will study ways to select the best teacher for your spiritual growth and to find your soul group. You will also be introduced to the teachers of wisdom, the Masters of Life, who are working every moment to assist humanity to rise into the light that is within. In the last chapter, you will begin to sound the note of your soul that announces how much light and love you have integrated in your life. This clear note can telepathically reverberate with clarity, power, and beauty, extending love to all around you.

Remember, when you are on your Bridge of Light, your soul creates fireworks of beautiful colors, dazzling sparkling stars, and intricate designs trailing like a comet across the sky of your horizon. Every action you take that is infused with this light has a powerful effect in the present, and it also streams its light into your future, awaiting your approach there so it may give its gift to you again and again. You stand in the middle between your past and your future; thus, you may not see these lines of light forming an arc over you, but they are there. Many of them are creating good fortune around you now. The essence energy of many wise thoughts and acts from your past is shooting lines of light into your future.

Chapter 14
Living From Free Choice

What makes the upcoming period of history so unique is that the new higher vibrations offer as much freedom as each person is willing to take responsibility for handling. The old system of following the authority of others is phasing out as new points of light appear in every area of living. For thousands of years, the culture has taught that people have little free choice, that they are victims of circumstance and can't do anything about it. Most people automatically adopted the philosophy of the people around them, accepting these cultural beliefs without question. Yet there were always a few people who awakened from the spell of "victim" superstitions to create empires, explore new continents, launch people into space, and dive into the depths of the ocean while everyone else declared it couldn't be done. In the new intensity of light, each of you can explore your own continents within the vast panorama of higher consciousness, launch yourself into the interstellar space of awareness, and dive into the depths of new understanding.

Your Basic Freedom

The most basic freedom on this planet is to keep moving into a higher vibration from which to live. Light is synonymous with change. Just as the energy of the universe is always changing and moving, creating one form and then another in its play, your life reflects changing ideals, ideas, and physical forms. When you consciously choose the ideals to live from, you are taking charge of your own evolution. Your ideals determine all other choices. Life and death, the purpose of life, what has value to you and what does not, what is essential and what is not, what is a backward step and what is a forward step—all these beliefs influence your future. Until now, people could drift along for years without much thought about their deeper beliefs. The deeper beliefs were there, but they were underground, beneath their conscious awareness. People rarely changed their beliefs. When you open to new light, you discover that the real purpose of your lift begins to shift.

Watch where people put their time and energy, not what they say, in order to ascertain their deepest beliefs about life. When you find someone who claims to be a student, yet is clearly living in profound wisdom and love, learn all that you can from that person. Doctrines are less important than sharing experience, knowledge, love, and joy—the greatest gifts older souls can bestow.

Finding Your True Responsibilities

Acting responsibly is choosing from your highest wisdom. You may sometimes feel confused about what is your responsibility and what you are doing out of a false sense of obligation. If you keep commitments that are in line with your understanding of your life's higher purpose, you are acting responsibly. A sense of obligation implies a burden, something that has been imposed from the outside, whereas responsibility comes from a commitment that you have freely chosen from the wisdom of your heart and mind.

There's one sure way to tell the difference between obligation and true responsibility. Obligation continually feels like a burden. If you feel obligated or dutiful, or find you have slid into something without checking your intuitive knowing, you may feel weighted down, burdened. Where you have submitted to what someone else thought you should do, old patterns of feeling like a victim could come up. It's easy to feel passive or helpless in the face of difficulty when it seems that the project or relationship was someone else's idea. On the other hand, handling true responsibility feels like a privilege. You may be working harder than ever, but you are doing what you do because you absolutely believe in it. Stand on your Bridge of Light and review all of your responsibilities in the illumination of your soul. When your energy, time, and money all go where your heart and mind agree, you are freely choosing your life.

You can discern which jobs, relationships, and homes you have chosen from your Essence Self because if they temporarily entail hard work, you find you don't mind the extra push. When any decision is made from the heart, there is an abundance of energy available to carry it through. Once you have determined your true responsibilities, you can use your energy to experiment with your highest visions and put your whole self into a new job, a new city, a new relationship, or the decision to have a baby or be a loving parent. If you are challenged by problems as you begin to carry through with the changes you have chosen, you may start blaming yourself for mistakes. Just remember how it felt as a child learning to ride a bicycle. You could keep your balance only if you kept moving forward and focusing on balance. Living from free choice is like learning to ride a bicycle. Focus on what is working, and you can expect delightful surprises while you are learning how to handle greater freedom of choice.

Choosing the Lighted Way

The only way a choice is a free choice is to choose with light. Choosing light means finding the highest, most light-filled way to relate to everything in life—jobs, friends, and family. A good preparation when you are thinking of changing jobs, relationships, or cities is to consider all of your choices. Note which ones tend to energize you when you think of them and which ones make your energy drop. If the choice feels light or seems to have a special shimmer around it, this choice has a good chance for the success you are visualizing.

If you feel yourself to be trapped in a situation, ask yourself this question even if you don't think there is an answer: "If there were a way to make this job (relationship, family, or school) into one I would enjoy, what would it be?" Often you can make new arrangements that work for all concerned, especially when you know you have a choice of staying or leaving. The same is true of a relationship. If you feel guilty and unhappy every time you are with the other person, for example, think of it as an opportunity to bring a much finer light into the relationship. One woman whose husband had decided they didn't have a real marriage anymore due to her intense interest in meditation brought so much light and harmony into her personality that they now have a spiritual marriage that is the best relationship they can imagine. Her husband has joined her meditation groups and is expanding his spiritual knowledge rapidly.

As you consciously choose the reality by which to view your life and the world about you, think about how you would tell your life story to someone you don't know. How would you tell it differently to your mother? Your children? Your friend? It is possible to look at your life as a struggle or to look at the very same life as one in which an incredible number of blessings are showered upon you. The circumstances can be exactly the same, and two opposite viewpoints can be seen as equally true. It depends on the thinker's choice of interpretation.

The Lighted Interpretation

By taking the stance that you are growing spiritually with each choice and change, you will indeed make that belief a reality. Two people may have the same changes happening to them, in their relationships, their jobs, or their financial base. One feels shaken and resentful and keeps replaying how he or she can get the old circumstances back again, while the other one focuses on the new opportunities presented. Even if a little fearful, the second person feels like a pioneer, confident that his or her Higher Self will lead him or her into the right circumstances and to the right people.

With your mind receiving more illumination and learning to hold steady in that light, you can identify beliefs that have caused unhappiness or apathy. It is possible to feel trapped or weighed down with obligations, or to feel honored to have these responsibilities – without a single change in the external situation. You may decide that you are being shaped into a powerful, compassionate, and loving person by each one of these responsibilities.

Your new experience comes from an inner change of perspective. An unloving partner can easily turn from a frog into a prince or princess if you begin to perceive him or her from a soul level and sense the inner radiance of his or her heart. A frog can also turn into a prince or princess when someone truly sees him or her as a noble being of love in his or her Essence Self.

As you realize your freedom to choose your life direction, you can see how important it is for you to give the people who are close to you the same freedom to choose their life directions. Your freedom to learn from your experiences and to take responsibility for each action opens your mind and heart to allow friends and family to take full responsibility for their lives as well. You may enjoy watching others discover the sovereignty of who they are, free to choose, to learn from their choices, and to choose again—just as you are doing. This is the path to mastery. If, for example, you see a better way for friends to be successful, assume that they are learning precisely the skills that will most benefit them now. What you see is how you would handle the situation if you were in it. Their skills and experiences are different from yours. But you can help them to see their choices more clearly by spinning a Bridge of Light to wisdom, bringing them onto this bridge, and allowing the pure light to permeate both of you.

A Journey to Experience Lighted Choices

1. As you approach your Temple of Light, create a quiet mind so that you can decide wisely what you wish to take re-

sponsibility for. Imagine that on the front door of the temple, beside your name, is carved the phrase "Freedom to Choose," and walk through the door into your temple. Think of how inherently free you are in mind, spirit, and body; be aware that no one can control your life without your agreement.

2. Look at one of the responsibilities in your life. See if it is from free choice. Does it fit your personal philosophy now?

3. Create a triangle of light to this situation. One point of the triangle of light emanates from your heart, one from the wisdom within your head, and the third point from the situation itself.

4. Breathe in with full trust in the power and love of your God within. Intensify the lines of light flowing through this triangle to transform the situation. See fine luminous strands of light pouring into your triangle. Say to yourself: "I am free. I am free. I am free to live from the wisdom and the authority of my divine Self. I am free to fully engage in the responsibilities that are mine, to experience joy over worry and love over fear."

5. Repeat these statements again and again until all the parts of your personality accept the idea.

6. Imagine that this freedom is being energized and that the results will be even better than those you are picturing—positive and powerful in adding light to your life and the lives of others.

7. Each time you think of this triangle of light, it becomes more potent to transform the situation at hand. Many new options are likely to appear in your mind over the next few days after you form this triangle of energy. This clearer picture of your new options will empower you and your work.

Chapter 15

Changing Your Past
to Change Your Future

Each of you has several potential futures already forming. One of these futures is the most likely to happen. Its probability is determined by the image that you now have of who you are—your memories of successes, failures, attributes, strengths, and weaknesses. To change this image of yourself, you can relive a past experience through the new lens of what could have happened if greater wisdom, compassion, and understanding had been available.

The process of loosening a memory and creating a new one is simple. The glue that holds your memories in place is light soluble. Just as water-soluble glue dissolves when water is applied, memory-holding glue dissolves when light is applied. You connect the memory to your Bridge of Light and let it illumine the negative pattern and dissolve it. Next, you replace it with a new memory, which feeds the subconscious mind with positive energy. Thus, your most probable future is lighted and expanded.

Since the subconscious mind does not make a distinction between an actual experience and an imagined one, you are erasing a negative picture and replacing it with a new one. You have done this many times—relived and reinterpreted or selectively remembered parts of an event in the past that enriched and empowered you. This skill in memory selection helped you get where you are now, but you may not have realized the wisdom in the process.

Creating New Memories

When you create memories of being wise and loving, your life becomes more flexible and open. As you change even one memory, your life immediately shifts to accommodate this new reality and your sense of Self becomes stronger. What used to seem like the only choice opens to new choices as you shift the original memory to a more empowering one. Automatic reactions to someone else, such as trying too hard to please, can now start dissolving. Where you said yes, you may now say no without apology or stress. Where you put off something important, you may now handle it with ease. Where you said no to yourself or to others, you may now say yes—and mean it.

Rather than look back with regret or guilt at something you did or an unwise choice you made, ask yourself if you consciously thought of a better choice and decided to take the second-best choice. Considering all of your experience, all of your hopes and fear, all of your beliefs and goals, you may see that you always made the best decision available at the moment. Now, after the experience of learning, and with the illumination on your Bridge of Light, you may naturally see a wiser choice in many situations of the past. You are ready to build the new choice into the situation as soon as you acknowledge sincerely that you did the best you could at the time. This acknowledgment is the first step toward releasing the biting sting of guilt or anger over something out of the past.

146

In the higher frequency of light, unresolved conflicts from the past get stirred up. Fortunately, any anger, resentment, guilt, or jealousy still hanging around from the past can be changed. You only need to know how to use light to change the memories that have caused you unhappiness, clearing your energy field for your new future. You can change the persistent little voice that criticizes you to a voice that supports you and enriches your future.

Infusing Solar Light

All of your experiences have brought you where you are now. There was something in every experience you have had that has served as a catalyst to move you forward and expand your idea of life. Each experience, from the best and the worst, brought you closer on the journey to the soul. When you fully realize this and build in the qualities with Solar light to these past experiences that you needed (but did not yet have), you can change the memory. After you have changed these memories to include positive outcomes, you may suddenly begin to remember a wealth of other experiences that were quite wonderful just as they were. The positive memories tend to get buried under the negative ones, and the wonder of releasing past memories of unhappiness is that the future shifts so rapidly to fit the newly created "past."

You can transform any memories of the past. After some practice with the less intense ones, you can work with major traumas. You can also create memories of being organized, clear, and powerful in your work as well as relationships, building these qualities into a specific time and place. Sometimes the transformation happens immediately. The painful

147

feeling that went with the memory is gone. You may even be left with a kind of silly feeling that you let yourself suffer over something like that. At other times, the process is more gradual, as the negativity slips away layer by layer.

After connecting the light of specific spiritual qualities to a memory and then reliving the new memory, you have made a shift in your future. The experience that you worked on will spread to other experiences in your past where you needed these qualities, and in time you may notice that life brings you many delightful experiences in which you use the soul qualities that you have added to your past.

The following process is powerful. Plan some undisturbed time. If you choose to do it, take notes so that you can acknowledge later the way you have enriched your future by transforming the past experience from a negative one to a positive one.

Changing an Unpleasant
Memory to a Pleasant One

1. If you want to release a hurt, loss, guilt, or regret from the past, select a memory of an event that is still somewhat unpleasant when you think of it. Find a symbol to represent this memory—a rock or a piece of driftwood, for example. Later, after you are more skilled, you can choose a more unpleasant memory.

2. Begin by breathing slowly and deeply. Then, sounding the sacred word OM, enter your temple. Align with your soul via your Bridge of Light.

3. Decide what soul qualities, if they had been available to you at the time, could have created a pleasant experience in that situation. Take time to feel the energy of these qualities

flowing into you. Select three of these qualities and place them at the points in a triangle (wisdom, love, and humor, for example). Now place the symbol in the center as shown:

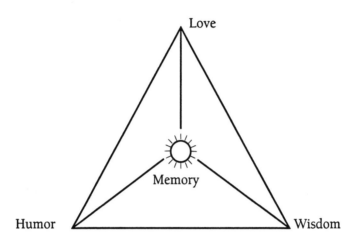

4. Draw a laser line of light from each of these qualities to the symbol in the center and let them permeate the symbol, irradiating it with their dynamic energy.

5. Spend several minutes doing this. Your symbol will begin to change as its molecular structure shifts to carry more light.

6. Think of the event now. Notice the action you would have taken to create a positive experience—lighter, more understanding, and pleasant! In any case, you may see the whole experience in a different light.

Chapter 16

Finding Where to Place Your Light

There is so much light permeating your mind that now the dilemma is what to do with all the light. A century ago, even a generation ago, it took years to tap into the light because of the density of the Earth, but now so much light is entering the earth plane that it happens quickly: You tune to it, open to receive it, and it comes pouring through.

Each soul reflects different aspects of the one Great Light. As you awaken to a greater purpose in being on this planet, you may feel drawn to learn everything you can about certain subjects. Perhaps you see your purpose to be developing a wise and complete understanding of life so that you can teach and illumine others. Or perhaps you sense that your purpose is to develop a deep, intuitive, loving understanding of people so you can nurture them and help them unfold their highest potential. If these purposes are close to your personality goals, you may have already noticed how expanded your heart feels when you hear of someone's suffering. You may be feeling an intense desire to reach out to help, but perhaps you don't know where to begin.

You may sense that your purpose is to serve God, or your highest ideal, with complete faith and utter devotion. Or your purpose may be to live with commitment, true to your highest vision of what is right. You may aspire to become a dynamic, powerful leader, serving the greatest good or working to liberate people from oppression. Or perhaps your purpose is to learn truth through deep thinking and careful reasoning. Another possibility – you may be most fulfilled putting practical, progressive ideas into action and seeing them through until they are well established.

Once you decide on the general area that you are most drawn toward, look for different ways to express this purpose. For example, if you are intrigued by the possibilities of bringing conflict into harmony, you might choose to work through music, art, family life, science, or religion. The divine quality of harmony shines through each soul differently. Even when many people are expressing harmony through a single art form, say sculpture, each produces unique results and reveals a different facet of harmony.

Suppose one thousand people decided to express spiritual harmony and higher truth through writing. Each one would create a rhythm and style to express his or her own highest vision of truth; because of individual training, culture, and different personalities, the variety would be very rich. Each would carry another facet of light into form and would attract the readers who resonated to that particular level, rhythm, and style of writing. Yet all the spiritual books are part of the larger purpose of bringing light to the minds of all humanity.

You may find that you are already expressing some part of your purpose very elegantly. You may be teaching and yet you do not think of yourself as a teacher. You may think that you are just talking with friends, yet you may be having a profound influence on their ability to connect with their Higher Self. Or you may be studying spiritual wisdom or

getting training in practical aspects of carrying out your purpose – for example, through computer literacy. Expressing
your purpose can depend on how well prepared you are to do
so. The subjects that you feel an inner urge to study may turn
out to be important skills when you find the form to express
your soul purpose.

It is far more energizing to choose one area of work that
gives your life the greatest meaning and to begin focusing on
that area than to try to cover several areas. Look first into the
area where there is the greatest need in which you have some
knowledge and skills. For example, if you have experienced
a great deal of conflict in your life, you have probably learned
important skills in creating harmony out of conflict. You may
be able to move quite naturally into facilitating and teaching
skills of working in harmony to individuals, families, and other
groups.

Once you are clear about your higher purpose, help will
come to you from many directions. You may be in night classes
with your inner teacher. When you are sleeping, you are out
of your body and can learn quite rapidly without interference
from your personality. In addition, new people may come into
your waking life to help. They may come from every walk of
life to teach you. Some will help you clear old beliefs that are
unproductive, even when they do not realize what they are
doing. Others whom you know or meet will openly support
your enthusiasm and new ideas.

When Daily Activities Count

Test every action you take, even small ones, and see
if they reflect your life purpose. Waiting for a bus, cleaning

up the kitchen, or shoveling snow off the drive—no matter what you are doing—try asking yourself, "What is the point of what I am doing right now? How does this fit into my larger purpose?" If it fits, a vitalizing energy will flow through your body. Even if what you are doing at the moment is simply taking care of the practical side of living, notice how this also supports your purpose. These activities are part of the responsibility of living on this planet as you expand your awareness and begin to express your real purpose. You can eat, sleep, work, play, and even laugh while you are simultaneously aware that you are absolutely on target with your purpose.

If you have a period in which you feel ambivalent about what to study, organize, or do next in expressing your purpose, first leaning one way and then another, imagine your life ten years in the future as it might be with each choice. The sense of adventure and high energy may be much stronger in one picture than the other. Go into your Temple of Light and mentally put one choice in each hand and notice which hand feels tingling and warm. This hand will be holding the choice where your energy is. Select the next step according to the greater sense of energy. Where your energy is, there will be your heart and highest joy—both the closest companions to your purpose.

Many people may soon experience periods of confusion, pulled between the old beliefs and the new. Their emotions can create a fog that temporarily confuses their minds. You can also serve from the inner planes by increasing the radiance of your Bridge of Light so that others may join you on your bridge and receive a boost of light, clarity, and compassion.

Focus your love and energy not on the people who are resisting the new incoming waves of light, but on those who are open and searching, who have already realized there is far more meaning to this life experience than the culture has taught. Whatever your vision is to help, when you reach out to others from your heart, you are serving a great need.

Recognizing Your Purpose

Every human being on this planet has a purpose. The masters and spiritual guides who are working with humanity need everyone, especially now, to help bring forth a new world order of freedom and love and light. A high vision reverberates with your heart and mind. It energizes you and draws you toward what you envision. As you connect your vision with this light, you may get a flood of new ideas. How do you choose the best one? How do you move forward to realize your vision? What can you do right now?

Your true vision will resonate with your desire to serve humanity, draw forth your inner truth, and strengthen your commitment. Too grand a vision must be cut into smaller chunks before it can be implemented. Too small a vision will leave you without inspiration or enthusiasm. Ask for a vision that matches the power and the light of your soul. No one can tell you what that vision should be. You are its sole creator. At first, you may get only a hint of it, or you may be puzzled by a symbol that comes to you, but each session in quietness and solitude assists you to discover another piece that is needed. Ask your Higher Self to make it clearer, to refine it, and to show you how to manifest it.

Give yourself several weeks of focusing on your purpose. Write a description of your highest possible future at the end of each week. Writing it tends to activate deeper levels of knowing. Observe how your experiences so far in life have prepared you to fulfill this purpose, even if you didn't know it at the time.

Developing Skills to Match Your Vision

Writing in a journal or writing an article for publication can help you get very clear and organized with your thoughts and plans about how to manifest your vision. It can also expand your contacts beyond those who live in your immediate area. Here is an opportunity for you to set personal ambition aside while you simply reach out with a message of the reality of the soul and the knowledge that is available in the light.

Do not count on anyone coming forth to furnish what is missing to manifest your vision. This expectation has stopped more light workers than almost anything else; they miss the urgency to develop the skills that their vision calls for in order to actually develop their vision. Learn the skill of making connections, organizing and getting people to work together, communicating by computers, and attracting money for higher purposes. These skills are important in manifesting almost any vision. You won't be doing it single-handedly, but the ability to understand and use money wisely is necessary in order to attract money; the skill of organizing allows you to delegate or share responsibility. Be alert for others you can work with who share a similar vision.

Become an expert in one major field of service. Think of the preparation as part of your purpose, but beware of delaying your work on the physical plane indefinitely out of false humility. If you wait until you know everything there is to know about your field of work—or if you wait for enough money, for the right partner, or your true teacher—your part in the great work for transformation might remain on the sidelines when you are truly needed and are ready to go to work.

The Dynamic Power of Focus

It is important to establish yourself in the field that you are most strongly attracted to even if you have a strong interest in several. What is on target as a purpose for one person may be a distracting activity for another. Your vision may be one of working with people to help them achieve healthier physical bodies while someone else's path is to work for children's rights. Someone working to establish laws to protect the environment could be spreading his or her energies too thinly by also working to free global political prisoners. If your main purpose is working with alternative schools, spending time on nutritional research could be off purpose for you.

Build a Bridge of Light to wisdom or clarity. Let its energy flow into any problem area that is presenting a block to your vision. Ask your Higher Self, "How can I use this situation to further my highest purpose?" New ideas may suddenly seem obvious and offer you choices that were not available to you before. The ideas you contact from your bridge are a direct connection to how to make your vision happen.

Your time is your life—counted out in segments. Spend your time as consciously as you spend money. Each week you have exactly 10,080 minutes. The richest, most powerful person in the world has not one minute more. Ask yourself frequently, "Is this the best use of my time and my life?" Put this question on cards. Keep one by the phone, one in every room of your house, one on your automobile dashboard, and one in your office. Within a few weeks, your time will seem to expand quite magically.

Think of your future as one of increasing levels of joy. The idea that expansion comes through suffering and that service comes only through dutiful sacrifice is no longer appropriate for the higher vibration of energies. The keynote of this planet is joy. Reflect deeply on the joy that you can bring to the world as your gift through the work that you want to do.

A Journey to Find Your Purpose

Choosing an area of service that most clearly resonates within your heart and mind adds meaning and joy to your life. Take a few minutes to become so clear that you can describe your purpose in life as you see it now, even though you do not know the form it should take.

1. Take three sheets of paper and copy one of the questions below at the top of each sheet. Then sit in silence and calm your mind. It's helpful to let go of the day's focus on work and let a sense of serenity permeate your body. Sound the sacred word and move into your Temple of Light. Experience the silence and begin to build the bridge or channel through which to see where you can make the most significant contribution to humanity. Then answer these questions:

- What do you want to know and understand more than anything else in the world?
- What is of the greatest value to you on this planet?
- What vision causes your heart to open and embrace life?

2. These answers may help to reveal your life's purpose. If you are not truly inspired by a sense of purpose, imagine that you have exactly nine full and healthy months of life left to express the most important thing in your life. Plan what you would do in these nine months. What would you do right now?

A Journey to Fulfill Your Vision

It's one thing to know your purpose and another thing to actually take action on it, or to expand the action you are already taking—and to do it with real joy. Here are the steps that we present to people in the Bridge of Light seminars.

1. In your Temple of Light, tune to the vibration of your purpose, the power and the beauty of it, until you feel its vitalizing energy. Make this feeling the basis of your vision for the future.

2. Imagine how you will feel, how your life will be different, and what you will see when you manifest your vision. The vision doesn't need a rigid form at this stage while you are gathering new energy and stability. If your vision is capable of taking you to your highest possible future, you will feel a definite stimulation in your heart as you think of it.

3. Create a movie in your mind of yourself walking into a room where you will learn what you need to know. See yourself with a very special book of spiritual laws under your arm. Step into your movie and actually experience the weight of this book in your arms, the weight of the door as you open it, and your delight as you take a place at the front.

4. As you walk into your movie, keep in mind your higher purpose of being a healer, teacher, scientist, educator, communicator, writer—whatever field you are most drawn to. Keeping your eyes focused on the higher path moves you into a

vibratory pattern that joins you with all true servers—your own kind of people. They share love, understanding, knowledge, and wisdom.

5. Imagine a few immediate, practical steps you can take to show your Higher Self that you are serious. You may be surprised at how much you can do now. A phone call or a letter to a friend or a group may be the first step. Schedule time for taking this step within the next week or so, and write this intention on your calendar.

Chapter 17

Energizing Your Physical Body

This chapter gives you some ideas on how to energize your physical body. Opening to finer frequencies of light through meditation requires an increasingly healthy and vital body. There are demands on your body that weren't there before. All of the powerful inner work you are doing—spinning Bridges of Light, bringing in the light of your soul, coaching subpersonalities to support your spiritual advancement—requires an extraordinarily clear and focused mind. The expansion that is taking place in your mind calls for an equal upgrading of the cells in your brain. You may already be less tolerant of low-quality food, alcohol, and drugs. As your body is upgraded, it may react very quickly to fraudulent foods that offer no nutritive value and tell you so by initiating a time-out for recovery when you do not honor its needs.

For an in-depth study of how to regenerate and heal yourself, how to bring your body and cells into the higher state needed to handle all the light you are bringing in, read Book II in the Awakened Life Series, *Healing With Light*. This is a practical and very informative book on how to grow spiritually without unnecessary suffering mentally, emotionally, or physically. You will learn where diseases begin and how to become immune to them. You will go to the Island of Regeneration and

CREATING YOUR HIGHEST POSSIBLE FUTURE

work from the seven rooms of the Temple of Healing with the healing angels and your own Solar angel. You will learn how to upgrade your physical, mental, and emotional bodies so that they become excellent instruments for your soul, not only now, but throughout your long and active life.

Finding Lighted Foods

Each time you go into your Temple of Light, you bring a finer submolecular substance to your body. This substance builds higher quality cells that create a resonance between your body and higher energies. These cells thrive and grow only on food that is fresh and pure, particularly food that still has a living essence. Until you become sensitive to this life essence, you can judge from the colors of food. Green foods, for example, vibrate with a purifying energy, helping to excrete toxins built up over the years. Orange fruits and vegetables build a very fine cellular structure. Golden fruits and vegetables supplement the spiritual vibrations flowing into your eyes and head. Organic food may have the greatest nutritive value. Add beans, rice and other grains, fresh nuts, and grain bread to the fresh green, golden, and orange vegetables and fruits, and you have a diet that will build a vitally alive and resilient body. These are the general principles of healthy eating. Study the latest research and have blood tests with professional healers to learn your body's individual needs.

Many foods have enzymes and antibodies that strengthen your immune system and build a net around invading bacteria to prevent them from getting established in your body. If you have eaten food or drunk substances in the past that compromised or weakened your immune system, the toxins produced are carefully stored and separated in a special place in your cells. You can learn how to develop a strong immune system and then safely flush these out through meditation, diet, and exercise.

Your New Physical Body

Toxins in the atmosphere can be released naturally and gently from your Bridge of Light. A natural flushing takes place, much like the flushing that occurs with niacin intake. The difference is that niacin works aggressively to flush out physical toxins, and soul light flushes out toxins from the etheric body, which in turn purifies the physical body.

You may see how important it is to purify the etheric body since it is the intermediary between your soul and physical body. The etheric body interpenetrates the physical body through millions of tiny filaments of light. It is the true source of physical health and longevity. As it becomes strong and purified, the etheric body protects, energizes, and rebuilds your physical body. You can feel the boundary of this body a few inches out from your physical body when you place your hand near someone's back at one of the points where the major energies converge and cross into the dense physical body. The other person can feel the presence of your hand touching the vital body. These are called energy centers, and you may know them as the chakras at the base, sexual, solar plexus, heart, throat, third eye, and crown centers.

The more you work with light, the more important it is for you to know how to distribute this light. Otherwise you may experience congestion in your body systems. If this happens, you can reestablish the connecting links of light and help distribute it throughout your body. For example, if you work with your hands, writing or healing, you may find some of this energy congested in your arms, shoulders, and neck. The secret is to keep the energy moving. Play with graceful and open free-form movements during frequent breaks, such as free-form dancing to beautiful music to move this energy.

To set up harmony with the higher vibration of light and support you as a spiritual being, you need everyday contact with this life spirit. As you increase the flow of your soul's light and energy, your etheric body becomes brighter and more efficient. The etheric body brings down the higher light and makes it available for the physical body. The regenerating energy of your soul circulating through your etheric body gradually shifts the note of your overall physical self to a higher note and has an effect on the people around you.

Building in Solar-Lighted Cells

When you meditate with your soul, imagine new cells of greater vibrancy replacing old ones. Let gratitude rise up from your heart for the opportunity to purify your body of all that is not in harmony with your spirit. This greater light builds a new body, one that is youthful, vibrant, and flexible.

Cells of higher quality bring youth to the body and are not subject to disease. The finer atoms, which are attracted to your energy field when soul light is flowing in, form cells that are resistant to common diseases. They regenerate your systems, especially the circulatory, respiratory, and nervous systems. When these key systems are vitalized, the other systems tend to become stronger as well.

Begin to observe your eating habits and the addictions

that were unconsciously given to you as a small child by your parents. Clearing up an addiction to sugar, for example, can add many years of a vital life energy. Addiction is the repeated indulgence in anything that your better wisdom tells you is not good for you. Your conscious intervention is essential, as you take the side of the Solar-responsive cells and starve out the low-vibrating cells that crave sugar.

As you provide nutritious food for Solar-lighted cells, along with giving them the rest and exercise they need and feeding them soul light every day, in a few months time you may experience a noticeable difference in your clarity and stamina and a greater ability to communicate with your soul.

With this increased sensitivity, you won't need to wait until physical symptoms warn you of danger ahead; you can become so sensitive to the laws of spiritual vitality that you take wise action before any physical problem appears and interferes with your spiritual path.

By building in Solar-lighted cells, there is less likelihood of having to take time out to take care of your body. You can experience vitality and energy with very little effort as your cells support the rhythms of living that are ever closer to your soul's rhythm. These will develop in stages as you work with sides of your personality, which may at first be confused by, and thus resistant to, the focused, smooth, and graceful rhythm of the soul.

Preparing Your Body to Hold More Light

Some people believe that if people are ill they must have fallen off the spiritual path, perhaps lost contact with the soul. Yet mystics and saints of the past have suffered physical illness, and numbers of spiritual leaders have suffered diseases. The ancient wisdom tells us that disease is inherent within the atoms that compose the human body. But the body is generally vulnerable only to these bacteria (which are harmless in small numbers) when the immune system is weakened through overwork, worry, and anxiety, or through lack of good nutrition and rest.

If you are ill, it is important to recognize that the cause is more likely to be that you have received too much light *before* the body was prepared to handle it – the very opposite of not having enough light. As the rays of light become more intense on this planet, they first affect those who are the most sensitive. This is why it is important to think of your body as an instrument of your soul and to upgrade its quality continually. Being sensitive to your body and taking care of it are small commitments to make in return for the rapid spiritual progress that is now possible. Think about these principles and then make a clear decision to start preparing your body to handle more light. This decision means that you are stepping up the reserves in your cells, that you are regenerating your cells with top-quality nutrition and supplements if needed, that you are educating yourself about nutrition and exercise, and that you are getting enough rest so that the transformation of your body can take place naturally, free of disease and suffering.

A Celebration of Your Life Force

1. Ask your body's forgiveness for carelessly ignoring its true needs – through improper food, lack of sleep, rest, or exercise, and prolonged stress – and for blocking its smooth energy

flow. Make a commitment to increase the life spirit flowing into your body.

2. Acknowledge to your inner self that you are part of an abundant life force that is continually healing and regenerating your body. Visualize this life force flowing into each cell. A deep sense of gratitude makes its force stronger.

3. Run your fingers lightly over all the surface of your skin, as if you are bringing this life force into every pore. Slowly and gently stroke one arm, beginning with the shoulders and moving to your fingertips to release holding patterns. Now stroke the other arm so that it will be as long as the first one.

4. Go for an early morning walk and breathe in a new life force. Inhale the life force of all the trees and flowers you see. Embrace the trunk of a tree, touch its leaves or flowers, and observe a transfusion of energy. The larger and more beloved the tree, the more energy will surge through you.

5. Become aware of your feet as the feet of your soul. Notice the difference in your balance, the rhythm of your steps, and the grace with which you walk.

6. Play with a puppy, a kitten, or a friend's small child and observe the liberated life force flowing into that being. Decide to be as open to discovery, as delighted with simple adventure, and as flexible as that being.

7. Weave a luminous cape of many colors with your creative imagination, a hooded cape that is long and flowing. You are a worker in light—you may as well wear a cape of light as you walk on this planet. With your beautiful cape flowing, hold your arms up and out. Turn your palms toward the sun, and send a message of hope and joy to all people. Visualize each person awakening to create a cape of light, resplendent with regenerating life force.

Chapter 18

Finding Your Teacher and Your Soul Group

There are some important questions to ask yourself as you look for a spiritual teacher who can assist you on your path. Here are some suggestions and questions to ask yourself to help you decide who might be the best teacher to help you discern the progress you are making, to share the ageless wisdom with you in terms that make sense in today's world, and to help you focus more of your life in light.

You would be wiser to trust your inner guidance for your personal life than to place all of your trust in someone else's authority over your life. A wise teacher leaves you free to live your personal life as you wish. He or she may make suggestions occasionally but does not in any sense dictate what you must eat or wear, where you should work, or with whom you should live. There is an unspoken trust that whatever you do represents an expression of the highest light within you. Do you see the qualities of love and wisdom, harmony and beauty, truth and trust, joy and intuition (or other qualities that you want to develop more fully) in this teacher?

Listen to this teacher's voice – to its timbre, tone, and quality – and observe the effect in your body and emotions. Are there overtones that help harmonize and heal your mind and body? The human voice gradually becomes the voice of the soul as its light and love are brought into the life. These overtones cannot be imitated; they form excellent criteria for finding one who has achieved some point of balance and integration of soul light.

Does this teacher honor all paths and religions that are reaching toward God or to the light? An inclusive spirit is the goal for humanity now. The exclusive spirit ("only our group is divinely inspired") is outdated for spiritual growth; it has caused much suffering and destruction, and it still exists in a few groups.

Does the teacher try to appeal to the student's personality ambitions for power, status, or material wealth? There is nothing wrong with having these things, but they do not satisfy the heart. And the hunger in the heart and soul must be filled before personality ambitions can bring *any* true benefits of peace or happiness.

Do both your heart and head resonate with the truth of this teacher's message? The merging of the heart and head is the ideal catalyst for spiritual growth. Heart energy alone tends to be sentimental and ineffective; head energy alone tends to be separative and cold. The two together are dynamic catalysts to create an atmosphere for truth.

Once you have chosen a teacher, either internal or external, decide that you will bring your spiritual life into full flower, evolving and learning, loving and forgiving with a joyous recognition of yourself as essentially divine and immortal.

Finding Your Soul Group

You may be ready to meet others like yourself who are on a similar path, preparing to take their place as light bearers in the world.

Spiritual groups are being taught to set up a vortex of energy that brings the whole group into a higher vibration. When three or more gather in the spirit of love and merge their energy to become a conduit or channel for light, the combined group energy provides reception that is far more powerful than one or two can summon. The light pours into the inverted cone or "V" and is distributed according to each person's capacity to handle it. Each receives in abundance, but no one is burned from too much light. Any surplus is distributed among the others. The more the group is focused on giving light to humanity, the finer the channel it creates. Its members become transmitters of light and can affect many people.

The members of a soul group are of different types and ages. They are drawn together because of a soul connection, usually from long ago. Look for agreement on the true group purpose in a soul group. This mutual purpose strengthens the ability of the group as an ever more useful and powerful instrument of love. A distinctive spirit of intelligent love and service becomes dominant as the group works together. A true soul group invokes light to flow into the minds of all people, love to flow into the hearts of all, and higher will and purpose to flow into the lives of all.

Some of the group are younger souls, less experienced than your soul, with a less developed love or less wisdom. Others in your soul group are older souls, experienced with more developed inner vision or understanding. When you find your soul group and have the opportunity to meet with this group on the physical plane, you may realize that you are modeling a wiser love with someone who is a younger soul than you at the same time you recognize someone who is demonstrating a greater heart and soul linking for you.

Linking With Your Soul Group

The light of the group soul is illumined each time a member consciously links with the group soul. Linking with the group from the inner plane is vitalizing to the spirit and illuminating to the mind. As the group works together, the members learn to handle destructive personality traits and tendencies to gossip and criticize with the light of the soul. These tendencies are recognized as the result of a personality temporarily disconnected from the soul. If members decide that the group direction is not in line with their higher purpose, they leave the group quietly.

Ask to find your true soul group, those who are consciously evolving toward enlightenment as you are. You may feel as if you are renewing some very old and wonderful friendships.

A woman who has made dramatic changes in her own life describes the group experience like this: "When I first walked into Jaiwa's seminar, I was a little scared as many others were. I had never done this before. But the moment I saw the faces of the people in the room, I felt a connection; it was a good feeling, like being with my family. Before each meditation and exercise, I asked to sense the purpose of the connection at this time with different people in the group. Sometimes I felt it in my heart, sometimes I heard words, sometimes I saw our connection in colors. It was phenomenal. Many of us had similar experiences. The bond grew deeper and deeper as we all allowed ourselves to reveal to one another what we were recognizing in the group. We were so happy that we started to acknowledge to one another, 'You seem so familiar; I have seen you on the inner planes.' We live in all parts of the United States, Canada, and Europe, and we meet as souls frequently now. We also gather on the physical plane at Jaiwa's seminars two or three times a year to continue our individual transformation work and to hold others in light. We meet together from the soul level with less interaction on the personality level. The power of our combined souls to reach and encourage others is much greater than any one of us alone."

Adding Light to Your Soul Group

This is an exercise to practice regularly as you begin to meditate. Your meditation is empowered with the light of the other souls, and your inner link on the higher plane offers more light to them.

1. With several deep, slow breaths, go to your Temple of Light and imagine that two or three other souls in or near your town are connected with you on the soul level. Even though you do not know who they are now, visualize these souls as points of light in the temple with you.
2. Form a circle with these points of light and visualize a greater light that embodies all of them. See your souls as points of light within a greater light.
3. Make three lines of light between each of these points. Let the first line be golden, the second line a deep royal blue, and the third line a beautiful shade of rose. Or choose other colors if you prefer.
4. Make a statement of intention to join with this group, such as "I join with each of you. May the love of my soul pour forth to you. May the ideas which my soul creates reach and encourage you."

5. Now hold this focus for a few minutes, and let the energy that you are sending forth resonate in these souls of similar vibration. Open to receive a response from these souls. This response is usually subtle, such as an energy lift or a feeling of happiness.

6. As the love of your soul reaches the minds of these people, you begin to set up a magnetic attraction to one another. Drop all expectations of who these souls are, and simply be alert to signals of an inner recognition from your higher mind and heart when you talk with people. In time, you will probably meet on the physical plane and recognize the energy of one another. Then you can work on the physical plane as well as the inner plane of awareness. Do not be surprised if more than two or three appear. Your soul is very inclusive and far-reaching.

Chapter 19

Preparing to Receive Your Master of Wisdom

The Masters of Life and Teachers of Wisdom (also known as the Shining Ones) are those who have attained total liberation from the physical plane, yet who have chosen, at great sacrifice, to assist humanity to transform the energy of Earth into a sacred planet where true spiritual joy is the dominant note in the musical chord of this planet. These masters have remained behind while other liberated souls moved on to a wider service, leaving this solar system completely or else working in one of its sacred planets. It is very important that you know who they are and that you understand something of the scope of their work.

These Masters of Life have been through every stage of humanity's school of evolution and have learned to use the laws of cosmic energy as a science in their unrelenting search for ways to reveal the greater purpose of life here and in the Universe. They work together to touch the minds of those groups who can receive from these higher frequencies of light – those who have purified their lives enough to use this knowledge effectively for the good of all humanity.

The Teachers of Wisdom do not consider themselves more spiritual than you. They see that all humans carry the spark of God within themselves. They are in a position to offer assistance because they have raised that spark to a pure white flame and because they understand the science of the soul after long experience with this plane. They have completed a deep study of the laws and principles of spirit and Earth matter. They can see more of the cosmic plan for humanity than those they teach.

The masters assist, yet they have no selfish purpose. On the human plane, there is a mix of selfish purpose with higher purpose. These teachers understand this, and they have no criticism. They wait patiently. They suggest new possibilities as they amplify the broadcast of the cosmic plan to bring humanity out of the shadowy cave and into light. The form you use to express this greater light and love is up to you. In this and the next cycle of humanity, the keynote of Earth, pictorially represented in the ancient records as joy, will bring peace and harmony to a long-suffering species that has been through great struggle.

In the past age, serious students found a master and put themselves in the master's hands, blindly obeying the master's authority, and hoping for personal liberation from this planet. Personal instructions from a master are now being superseded by group contact and training. One of the Teachers of Wisdom will recognize your group's growing ability to anchor greater knowledge here and will energize the group soul and its work.

Opening to Your Master's Light

When you have developed the inner unity of spirit with your soul group, the masters work with you through the group. They assist and teach all groups who are serving the cosmic plan to bring light and love to this planet. Many times, these groups have no idea their work is being energized by a master.

The Masters of Wisdom do not work with personalities; they work with the soul, which in turn trains the personality. Using a wise economy of energy, they delegate most responsibility for any individual teaching and training to their disciples. Each is careful to offer only the stimulation of light that the individual or group is able to handle. Since the changes must be made in a more or less sequential order and cannot all be made at once, they allow time between contacts for souls to integrate the light received and to prepare for the next stimulation.

At this time, none of the masters or their assistants, the higher initiates and angels, appear in a physical form except in very rare and extreme circumstances when it is absolutely necessary for their work. They work through the subtle planes and broadcast on certain wavelengths to further the progress of humanity. They broadcast to those who have built a strong bridge to the soul and desire to serve in some way. All work is done from the soul level to help reveal the next step in the cosmic plan for this planet. Each master works with some part of this grand design to bring great love and wisdom as the natural mode of expression on Earth.

As the masters work from the subtle planes to teach and assist their students, they may drop a suggestion into your mind, but your response is entirely up to your intelligent judgment and sound common sense. One of the assistants to your master (a spiritual guide) may work more directly with you and gently point out personality tendencies that you could shift into greater light. This is why there is such benefit when you create the Bridge of Light that links the personality with the Essence Self. Only when the personality and the soul have a strong link can the link with a master be made.

With the human race evolving so rapidly, there is a great need for teachers on the physical plane. Many teachers must be trained to fill this growing need. The cosmic plan is greatly accelerated when there are teachers who can teach through living the greater truth and expressing the higher spiritual purpose of life. Those who are being trained to teach spiritual truths are tested carefully. Be aware that you may be of great service in this field, and consider making the commitment to be trained as a teacher.

Perceiving Contact With Your Master

Even though the Teachers of Wisdom do not use a physical body, their light body is so radiant and their aura so intense that even a brief contact with them is a tremendous stimulus to your personality as well as your soul. You respond according to your own education, training, and background, and your soul and personality type.

You can create a sensitivity in your inner ear to be alert at all times for a signal from your master or one of your master's assistants. It may be an audio signal—a brief, high, yet very clear tone within your head. You may not hear anything, but feel an energy in the head that signifies the greater presence of the master. Or you may have an awareness of an extrasensory presence, a kinesthetic sense in your head and heart centers.

Do not be anxious about too much stimulation from the higher communities of light. They know each soul's capacity and adjust the light accordingly. Everything is done in graduated steps with great care. The problem with using any artificial means to open the doors of perception is that too many doors can open at once. The result is likely to be a mental overload followed by total exhaustion with no real gains of spiritual growth. The two worlds may be too widely separated for true integration of spiritual wisdom to take place.

The masters and spiritual guides send messages as thought waves on currents of nonattached love, an energy that is particularly healing and swift. Your Higher Self picks them up and proceeds to draw them down into your conscious mind, where they may seem like your own ideas. These times of great stimulation of light open doors that were not even present before.

The contact of a master is also possible at night while you are in deep sleep and out of your body. A dream, vividly impressed upon your mind, may tell you that an interview with your master has taken place. Upon contact with your master, even in your deep sleep, there is a unique stimulation of your mind, your emotions, and your sense of vitality.

Discerning Among Higher Impressions

Gradually, you will be able to discern if the impressions you are receiving are from your soul or from the teacher in your master's group who is assisting you. Begin to anticipate the possibility of receiving occasional contact or impressions from this group of teachers. If some part of your mind holds back to be sure that you are not being foolish or gullible, be alert to these signals and work with the subpersonality who holds you back until you gain its cooperation.

179

Being contacted by your master is very different from simply manufacturing a "guide" for yourself without having created a solid Bridge of Light to your soul first. It also is different from inviting any stray entity who might take advantage of a "come one, come all" invitation. There are many levels of beings who do not presently have physical bodies, just as there are all types of beings with physical bodies. Few people would be so foolish as to open their front door and invite every passerby to enter. Opening to receive information from higher sources is done from the safety of your Bridge of Light, as close to your soul as you can be.

You may have heard people talk about taking their guide's advice and quitting their jobs, leaving their families, and traveling around the world until their money ran out, and you may have wondered what kind of guide would set this up. The higher guides do not interfere with the details of your personal life; they respect your ability to listen to the whisperings of your soul. As you learn to discern the difference between your unconscious mind and a higher guide, you may have times of confusion. You might receive part of the guide's message clearly, but as you translate it into words, it may be mixed with unrecognized desires or beliefs from your own mind. When a desire is strong enough, it can seem that someone outside of yourself is urging you to do it. Be very skeptical about such urgings; they are probably coming from your own unconscious mind. If desires show good common sense with messages (such as "organize your time"), follow them carefully. These are the kinds of messages that very likely are coming from a higher guide.

One man in our seminar wanted his guide to direct his daily life and tell him what decisions to make about his personal life. Instead, his guide inspired him with creative ideas about how he could send a constant stream of love to flow over his town. Several of the group began to describe similar experiences, and they soon realized that by using their minds and their common sense, they were growing rapidly in their confidence to handle whatever came up. They admitted that they did not want to be treated as children and miss the opportunity to develop good judgment and wise timing through their own experience with their soul on the Bridge of Light.

We taught a group in one of our seminars to imagine an image of their master just above and between their eyes, about three or four inches out from their faces. Each one imagined a very small image of the master's face. Everyone experienced an inflow of energy from this very simple exercise.

Identifying Your Time of Preparation

1. Pretend that the date when you will receive a wonderful stimulation from one of the Teachers of Wisdom is already set and that it is up to you to be ready for this meeting, to have your body purified, your emotions and mind purified, your life and your surroundings cleared and organized. Imagine this date within one to twelve months and mark it on your calendar. Let this date motivate you to get your life in order and eliminate nonessentials that take up time and energy yet do not truly serve anyone. Identify your true responsibilities, face them, and add such love and harmony to them that the power of the soul is demonstrated. Your true responsibilities are part of your spiritual work. Meeting them halfheartedly delays true progress. Meeting them wholeheartedly calls forth inspiration and divine love beyond all measure of receiving for the personal self alone.

2. How would you change your diet, exercise, and sleep schedule? How would you clear junk out of your house? Junk is anything that does not serve a needed function, including the function of beauty. As you recognize how much energy these unused and stored things are taking from you, you can pass them on to others. Each release promotes a light spirit as the part of your energy that was stored in these possessions is returned to you.

3. Next, see how many emotions are in your energy field that make you sad or mad. Imagine that you are in a cosmic store of "emotions" and select two or three that would most energize and give you joy. These will have a pleasing fragrance and taste, lifting you out of discouragement in the worst of times and offering you a joyful spirit in the best of times.

4. You may also become aware of how cluttered your mind is at times with thoughts that add very little light. Make a game of identifying these thoughts, and purposely substitute a more light-filled thought in its place. Denser thoughts tend to extinguish themselves when no attention is given to them, just as the light-filled thoughts will grow very strong when you play with them.

5. Keep your eye on the date you have chosen. Extend it if you need more time. The more serious you are, the more time you may want in order to be truly prepared.

Telepathic Receiving From Your Higher Guide or a Master

When a higher spiritual guide or a master contacts you or your soul group, you receive impressions in the form of an inner knowing or a deeper understanding. Even if your brain does not immediately translate the messages that are being received, they are impressed in your higher mind and will become clear to you over the next few weeks or so. Nearly always, you will perceive them as obvious common sense, something you see now which you somehow missed seeing before. You may find solutions to personal problems, not because the master solves them for you, but because your mind is flooded with so much light that you see for yourself the wise way to be. It is quite likely that you may feel rather enlightened for some time after a contact. You know, understand, and see much that was in a foggy cloud before.

It isn't always possible to track down each impression and know whether it came to you from your soul, a higher guide, or your master. There are many higher beings who are assisting the human race. They do not interfere with anyone's free will, because free will is part of the purpose of this planet's evolutionary system. They broadcast on a very clear station that is amplified by a column of light, and if you get to this particular vibration in which the broadcast is being sent out, you will be able to sense part or all of it.

This is the experience of a teacher who has been expanding her Bridge of Light for about one year: "I used to expect wonderful things to happen (when I meditated) and they didn't! I realized that I was starting off saying to myself, 'This isn't going to work; this isn't going to do anything.' But this summer I said to myself, 'No! This (spiritual work) is going to affect my life—because I intend it to do so.' I had a meditation yesterday that was incredibly beautiful and deep. There was so much love that it went way beyond being just me; I felt a partnership. When I used to meditate it was like a connection to a higher place, but now it feels like there is someone or a group there helping and working with me. I knew that before on a mental level, but now I have *experienced*

183

it, and it has affected me so much that I have this new sense of trust. I can hardly wait for the next day. Every time I meditate now, I am connecting with a higher being. I feel the connection of this being working somehow in my heart and in my mind. It's not like I see a being, but I feel the presence of one or more spiritual beings working with me in my life. I can't explain it because it is so new to me."

Evaluate each idea that seems to come from a guide or teacher, use your common sense above all, and act according to your best judgment. As you practice receiving impressions from higher sources of light, be aware of how easily illusory reflections of the higher world can be confused with true contacts with a guide. These illusions can be quite lovely, but they do not have any real substance or carry the power of light or transformation in them. The way to break through the fogs that distort the higher truth is to release any ego-based desire to be contacted by a master or guide. An intense desire can actually block your guide's ability to reach you. When you place yourself in the service of humanity and focus on learning what you can do to help, you start clearing all barriers that could prevent a clear and pure connection. One day you will realize that you are an active member of your master's group—and that you have been under your master's watchful eye for a long time.

Chapter 20
Sounding Your Soul's Note

We acknowledge you as a pioneer, courageously adventuring into greater light and preparing to help with the transformation of this culture to one of cooperation and positive intention. You now have the essential tools of light for your spiritual transformation. You have ignited the cool white flame of your soul in the center of your Temple of Light. You have constructed your Bridge of Light with streams of beautiful colors to many aspects of your soul; you have traveled into the center of spiritual courage, love, and joy, and brought many others to your bridge. You have examined personality goals in the light of your soul, breathed as your soul, begun to train and integrate your subpersonalities, faced your worst fears and challenges, recognized decision points as opportunities, and learned how to stay sane and balanced as you move into a spiritual life. You have begun to create your highest possible future through making choices as your soul, adding light to your past, energizing your higher purpose and your physical body, and finding your teacher and soul group. You have begun the preparation to work more closely with your Master of Wisdom.

You have been planting many seeds in your mind, emotions, and body as you have read this book. Much has happened without any effort on your part as you have read. Much more can happen now as you make a clear decision to continue the transformation that you have begun regardless of what may happen in your life. You are beginning to sound a new note in your life–the note of your soul. This is happening because you are gaining the courage to be all that you can be–and to be more tomorrow than you can be today. This is happening because you now know that you can reach out tomorrow to the soul awareness that may have been just beyond your reach yesterday. Your new note is sounding as you begin to establish closer contact with your soul and to bring its wisdom into your life now.

As you bring your life into the finer vibration of your soul, a harmonious inner sound goes forth, reverberating with joy. Your Bridge of Light will grow to become a Rainbow Bridge of Light, streaming with every color across the sky, broadcasting your soul note of joy. This joy surrounds you now! It vibrates through every human soul–waiting only for the touch of divine love to spring from its prison and add its note to the world. You can charge the atmosphere with this higher note, and when there are enough of you who are sounding these new notes, the right use of life force will overcome all that opposes it, and humanity will move closer to the door of initiation into a higher consciousness.

Living in the Soul's Open Spaces

There is an intense light in the center of your soul that is protected by several sheaths or petals, much as a rosebud. Your spiritual will to expand is the catalyst that will draw from your soul a greater flow of its powerful life energy to move through your whole being and vibrate so that the petals open. This process enables your soul to sound its new note through your life. It is this vibratory acceleration that will make this lifetime the one in which you can leave the small rooms of the personality and begin to live in the open spaces of your soul.

Behind you are countless experiences that have made it possible to connect with your soul now. All of the experiences of your life have brought you to this point of spiritual transformation. Every book you have studied, every teacher, every relationship, travel, project, thought, belief, and ambition you have had has projected you further on your path. Every teacher, every relationship, every home, every job, and every place you've traveled has provided a field of study for you to see your consciousness reflected in your surroundings. All of these have motivated and inspired you to begin this journey of spiritual transformation.

In front of you now are the opportunities to use every watt of the light you are bringing in. Make a promise to yourself that you will remember to turn to your Bridge of Light if and when a wave of confusion or anxiety threatens to loosen your anchor to your Bridge of Light. You need never be trapped again in any situation that casts a dark shadow on your life; you have the key to know the wisest steps to transform the way you see it and the way you handle it. You need never feel helpless again to do something about an unhappy life, to find the soul qualities needed to change it, and to take wise action with loving understanding. It is up to you now to build in these new patterns of soul light again and again until they become an invincible force that liberates you from any situation that cannot reflect the light of your soul. Your true freedom comes as you take full advantage of the opportunities that any conflict offers as it reflects and exaggerates an unconscious conflict within your psyche that becomes visible once outer conflict begins.

You Can Only Go Forward

Whatever happens, you will not ever need to turn back to the old ways of being. Regardless of how strong the temptation, you will recognize that something terribly important within you would die. You can only go forward, even if you get swamped with distractions occasionally. It is your ability to persevere, to start over any time you get sidetracked, that sets the progress you make in any one day, year, or lifetime. From now on, you can find a way to have the sun break through any clouds or storms in your life. As your personality becomes more flexible and far-seeing through the eyes of your soul, it will not need to cling to the old ways. You now have the tools to charge your personality with a renewed sense of spiritual adventure if needed, to teach it the release and delight that come when new ways are embraced—to think, to feel, and to act.

As you leave behind the distractions that once absorbed much of your time and attention and look to this future, you begin to know yourself to be an essential part of the whole, broadcasting the thoughts that your soul is creating: "We are in this together; we came to do this job; we came to learn to love, to create, and to work from the heart of the sun, the heart of God. From this place of pure love where we meet, we can help heal the fear that separates and divides our whole human race."

Let your compassion grow for all humanity. Look at the sea of humanity's faces and see all the suffering you have ever known reflected in their faces. See in their eyes the same despair you felt before you awakened and began to understand why you are here. Become your soul and sense its healing love lighting up their eyes and softening their faces. Dare to look and see the same transformation happening in your own eyes and your own face. No one can stop you but yourself. Remember to retrain any subpersonality who has followed those who speak with authority yet know little, or who has followed those who speak of hopelessness because they examine the world from a basement window.

Let the Spiritual Sun warm your wings and the spiritual air currents carry you into your highest future, and each spiritual seed will grow rapidly. Trust that the life energy of the spiritual seeds within your mind and heart is creating a beautiful life. Your trust encourages these seeds to sprout, grow, and bear fruit. It encourages the right use of your time and talents; it allows your soul to sound its note in the world. You cannot help but begin to recognize yourself as an integral part of the light of the world, a cell in the heart of God, and the heart of the Spiritual Sun—a volunteer in the seamless fabric of light broadcasting this regenerating energy to all life on this planet. You are strengthened immeasurably by this connection! You thus know your soul to be one among many others, joined as a dynamic force of light.

Become aware of countless points of light within a magnificent body of living, pulsating energy. Recognize your soul as one of these points of light, sounding its note, and adding to the infinite beauty and majesty of the World Soul. You can become a shining beacon for all those who are one or two steps behind you. Let the note of your soul ring out and join with the notes of other souls, creating a beautiful symphony of celestial music, offering all that you have and all that you know.

Remember, it is not only what you are doing, but the experience of joyous discoveries on your spiritual journey that marks a life of true value. If you embrace the divine love and profound awareness that are always available to you on your Bridge of Light, then any direction in which you move will bring joy and fulfillment.

May every blessing be yours!

Bridge of Light Meditations and Guided Journeys

Guided Journeys on Audio Cassette

Jaiwa has made two volumes of tapes to go with this book and help you to enjoy higher knowledge, joy, and courage as you move forward on your path. Sound—through voice, music, and higher binaural frequencies—can transmit extraordinary frequencies of spiritual transformation.

Bridge of Light, Volume I ($59.95)
Creating Your Temple of Light, Creating Your Bridge of Light, Bridge of Light to Courage, Bridge of Light to Love, Bridge to Light to Joy, Heart and Soul Connecting, Training Your Subpersonalities, Building Lighted Emotions. Eight guided journeys in stereo with angelic music and sound frequencies on four double-sided audio cassettes.

Bridge of Light, Volume II ($59.95)
Spiritual Trust, Bringing Conflict Into Harmony, Spiritual Choices, Changing a Memory, Creating Your Highest Future, Parts I and II, Sounding Your Soul Note, Joining Your Soul Group. Eight guided journeys in stereo with angelic music and sound frequencies on four double-sided audio cassettes.

(Volumes I and II are $99.95 when ordered at the same time.)

Your Temple of Angelic Healing, Volume I ($59.95)
Guided meditations for: A Journey to Your Temple of Healing, Connecting With Your Solar Angel and Soul, Healing With Your Golden Triangle, Healing With the Angels of Divine Love, Healing With Angelic Colors, Healing With Angelic Sounds, Learning From Your Inner Healer, Creating Your Healing Hologram. Eight journeys in stereo with angelic music and sound frequencies on four double-sided audio cassettes.

191

Healing Your Systems and Cells, Volume II ($59.95)
Guided meditations for: Regenerating Your Circulatory System, Revitalizing Your Nervous System, Purifying Your Respiratory System, Strengthening Your Immune System, Rejuvenating Yourself, Raising Cellular Light, Raising Your Will to Be Healed, Creating Your Highest Healing. Eight journeys with angelic music and sound frequencies on four double-sided audio cassettes.

(Volumes I and II are $99.95 plus shipping when ordered at the same time.)

Angelic Journeys for Special Healing ($29.95 each)
(Each volume contains four healing journeys on two double-sided cassettes.)
 Angelic Healing for Contagious Diseases
 Angelic Protection From Fears and Anxiety
 Angelic Healing for Pain
 Angelic Healing for Hospitals, Dental Visits, or Surgery
 Angelic Assistance for Autoimmune Disease
 Angelic Assistance for the Endocrine System
 Angelic Healing for the Digestive System
 Angelic Healing for the Muscular and Skeletal Systems
 Angelic Protection From Environmental Damage
 Angelic Healing for Accidents
 Angelic Healing for a Strong Heart
 Angelic Healing for Allergies
 Angelic Healing for Cancer

Revitalizing Journeys on Single Tapes ($9.95 each)
(The same journey is on both sides to replay without rewinding. Angelic background music and sound frequencies in stereo sound.)
 Revitalizing Yourself With the Angels (two voices, one for each ear)
 Angelic Healing for Awakening
 Angelic Healing for Sleep
 Angelic Healing for Headaches

Choosing Light Newsletter

To receive a free subscription to the newsletter with articles by Jaiwa and a description of all tapes and seminars, write to Choosing Light,

P.O. Box 804, Ashland, OR 97520. Include your name, address, and phone number.

Seminars

Jaiwa gives two weekend seminars near San Francisco each year. You will learn new processes for your journey of spiritual transformation, learn how to heal yourself, and meet new friends from many countries. Write for the dates and descriptions of these seminars.

The Awakening Life Series

Book II: Healing Yourself With Light:
How to Connect With the Angelic Healers
by LaUna Huffines
Publisher: H J Kramer

Healing Yourself With Light is an excellent companion book to *Bridge of Light* to take you to the next step on your path. Jaiwa guides you in connecting with the healing angels to build the colors and vibrations into your energy field that heal and raise the light in your cells. This strengthens your immune system to resist disease and illness. Once you begin building your Bridge of Light, your body needs cells tuned to a higher vibration—cells of greater light, longevity, and vitality. The new cells of finer molecular building blocks can receive and absorb much more light from your soul. Raising the light in your cells allows the great love and intelligence of your soul to flow into every cell of your body. It allows your brain to hold more light and translate the impressions being received from your soul.

In this book, you are met and taken to the Island of Regeneration and to the Temple of Healing. In the seven rooms of your temple, you meet and work with the healing angels. Through color, sound, and light patterns, these angels attract the atoms and molecules that build cells of greater longevity and vitality. You also meet and cooperate with the directors of your systems and learn how to purify your whole energy field. You communicate with your inner healer and learn what you can do to accelerate healing and evolve your body, and you build powerful images that empower you and strengthen your will to move ever forward on your path of spiritual transformation.

193

Choosing Light Order Form

Qty.	Description	Price

Postage Rates

Up to $35.00: $3.50 shipping charge.
Over $35.00: Add 10% of order up to $10.00.
Canada: Add $5.00 additional postage.
All overseas orders: Add $15.00 additional postage.
(If your order exceeds this postage, we will
notify you.) Orders shipped in 48 hours for an
additional $5.00. Call for rates on air delivery.
Regular orders shipped within 5 to 7 business days.

Subtotal	
Postage	
Priority handling ($5.00)	
Total	

Name _____

Address _____

City_____ State _____ Zip_____

Phone: Home ( ) _____ Work ( ) _____

Visa or MasterCard #_____ Exp. Date_____

Signature as on card _____

Make check payable to Choosing Light.

Mail order form to: Choosing Light, P.O. Box 804, Ashland, OR 97520

For credit card orders call (541) 488-1322 or fax (541) 488-0936

ALSO FROM H J KRAMER

HEALING YOURSELF WITH LIGHT:
How to Connect With the Angelic Healers
by LaUna Huffines
The complete guide to the healing power of light for physical,
mental, and emotional health.

RECLAIMING OUR HEALTH:
Exploding the Medical Myth and
Embracing the Source of True Healing
by John Robbins
In his rousing and inspiring style, John Robbins, author of
Diet for a New America, turns his attention to the national debate
on health care.

MESSENGERS OF LIGHT:
The Angels' Guide to Spiritual Growth
by Terry Lynn Taylor
Learn how to spot angels, communicate with them, utilize their
help, and love life the way they do.

CREATING MIRACLES:
Understanding the Experience of Divine Intervention
by Carolyn Miller, Ph.D.
Discover the book where science and miracles meet!
The first scientific look at creating miracles in your life. These
simple practices and true stories offer new wisdom for accessing
the miraculous in daily life.

THE LIFE YOU WERE BORN TO LIVE:
A Guide to Finding Your Life Purpose
by Dan Millman
Dan Millman's popular Life-Purpose System features key spiritual
laws to help understand your past, clarify your present, and change
your future.

If you are unable to find these books in your favorite bookstore,
please call 800-833-9327.

ALSO FROM H J KRAMER

THE ALCHEMY OF PRAYER
Rekindling Our Inner Life
by Terry Lynn Taylor
The Alchemy of Prayer is an original, inspiring, empowering, and loving look at a timeless subject by best-selling angel expert Terry Lynn Taylor.

TARA'S ANGELS:
One Family's Extraordinary Journey of Courage and Healing
by Kirk Moore
The singular account of a father's journey through grief and the awakening of the soul of a family to profound love and spiritual purpose.

UNDERSTAND YOUR DREAMS:
1500 Dream Images and How to Interpret Them
by Alice Anne Parker
The essential guide to becoming your own dream expert— makes dreaming a pleasure and waking an adventure.

INTO A TIMELESS REALM:
A Metaphysical Adventure
by Michael J. Roads
Australian author Michael Roads explores the links between nature, evolution, consciousness, and time. A riveting journey through realms of consciousness—a lesson in reaching beyond limitation.

THE LAWS OF SPIRIT:
Simple, Powerful Truths for Making Life Work
by Dan Millman
From the author of *Way of the Peaceful Warrior,* a book of timeless values, containing twelve universal principles for living and loving well.

If you are unable to find these books in your favorite bookstore, please call 800-833-9327.